Marilla D. Svinicki, *Univer*
EDITOR-IN-CHIEF

R. Eugene Rice, *American As. ... jor Higher Education*
CONSULTING EDITOR

Techniques and Strategies for Interpreting Student Evaluations

Karron G. Lewis
University of Texas, Austin

EDITOR

Number 87, Fall 2001

JOSSEY-BASS
A Wiley Company
www.josseybass.com

TECHNIQUES AND STRATEGIES FOR INTERPRETING STUDENT EVALUATIONS
Karron G. Lewis (ed.)
New Directions for Teaching and Learning, no. 87
Marilla D. Svinicki, Editor-in-Chief
R. Eugene Rice, Consulting Editor

Microfilm copies of issues and articles are available in 16mm and 35mm, as well as microfiche in 105mm, through University Microfilms Inc., 300 North Zeeb Road, Ann Arbor, Michigan 48106-1346.

ISSN 0271-0633   ISBN 0-7879-5789-5

NEW DIRECTIONS FOR TEACHING AND LEARNING is part of The Jossey-Bass Higher and Adult Education Series and is published quarterly by Jossey-Bass, 989 Market Street, San Francisco, California 94103-1741. Periodicals postage paid at San Francisco, California, and at additional mailing offices. Postmaster: Send address changes to New Directions for Teaching and Learning, Jossey-Bass, 989 Market Street, San Francisco, California 94103-1741.

New Directions for Teaching and Learning is indexed in College Student Personnel Abstracts, Contents Pages in Education, and Current Index to Journals in Education (ERIC).

SUBSCRIPTIONS cost $59.00 for individuals and $114.00 for institutions, agencies, and libraries. Prices subject to change.

EDITORIAL CORRESPONDENCE should be sent to the editor-in-chief, Marilla D. Svinicki, The Center for Teaching Effectiveness, University of Texas at Austin, Main Building 2200, Austin, TX 78712-1111.

Cover photograph by Richard Blair/Color & Light © 1990.

www.josseybass.com

Printed in the United States of America on acid-free recycled paper containing 100 percent recovered waste paper, of which at least 20 percent is postconsumer waste.

CONTENTS

FROM THE SERIES EDITORS

About This Publication. Since 1980, *New Directions for Teaching and Learning* (NDTL) has brought a unique blend of theory, research, and practice to leaders in postsecondary education. We strive not only for solid substance but also for timeliness, compactness, and accessibility.

This series has four goals:

1. To inform about current and future directions in teaching and learning in postsecondary education
2. To illuminate the context that shapes those new directions
3. To illustrate new directions through examples from real settings
4. To propose how new directions can be incorporated into still other settings

This publication reflects the view that teaching deserves respect as a high form of scholarship. We believe that significant scholarship is done not only by the researcher who reports results of empirical investigations, but also by the practitioner who shares with others disciplined reflections about teaching. Contributors to *NDTL* approach questions of teaching and learning as seriously as they approach substantive questions in their own disciplines, dealing not only with pedagogical issues but also with the intellectual and social context out of which those issues arise. Authors deal with theory and research and with practice, and they translate from research and theory to practice and back again.

About This Volume. The authors in this volume explore the difficult question of interpreting student feedback. All faculty have to be evaluated by students at some point in their careers; the value of the evaluation depends on both the students' ability to provide feedback and the instructor's ability to interpret it. Both are addressed by this volume.

Marilla D. Svinicki
R. Eugene Rice
Series Editors

MARILLA D. SVINICKI, editor-in-chief, is director of the Center for Teaching Effectiveness at the University of Texas, Austin.

R. EUGENE RICE, consulting editor, is director, Forum on Faculty Roles and Rewards, AAHE.

Editor's Notes

Student evaluations of teaching are used extensively throughout higher education; the faculty members whose teaching is being evaluated are often frustrated when they try to make sense of the numbers and written comments contained in these evaluations. Instructional consultants and faculty developers frequently hear remarks such as, "These student comments just don't make any sense. Some of the students say I'm wonderful, while others think I'm the worst teacher they ever encountered." The scholars and practitioners writing for this volume of *New Directions for Teaching and Learning* provide practical advice for faculty and administrators who are trying to make sense of the data gleaned from student evaluations or ratings. They bring information from the abundance of research that has been conducted on this topic and translate it into usable techniques and strategies.

In the first article, John Ory provides a somewhat humorous look at the popular myths surrounding student evaluations and cites research that provides insight into what is known concerning student evaluations and their use. Encouraging students to provide meaningful feedback is the focus of the article by Marilla Svinicki. One of the main problems cited about student ratings is that the students do not take them seriously and thus do not provide thoughtful and constructive criticism; Svinicki provides suggestions for alleviating this problem. The first of my two articles looks at student written comments and how faculty can organize them to provide usable feedback to improve their teaching and student learning.

Most faculty developers stress using midsemester feedback. In my second article, I look at some simple and more complicated ways to obtain meaningful feedback in the middle of the semester, while there is still time to make changes for the students in that class. Devorah Lieberman, Nancy Bowers, and David Moore offer suggestions about how to incorporate technology into midsemester feedback. Technology, they say, can give students more opportunities to provide input.

The next two articles provide techniques for getting feedback from groups of students rather than from individuals. Larry Spence and Lisa Lenze describe quality teams as a way to help teachers make the process of getting feedback more reflective and collaborative. Richard Tiberius relates a somewhat different group method for getting feedback by using focus groups. He has streamlined the process to make it more efficient.

Sometimes none of the questions on published student rating scales ask what faculty really want answers to. William Rando has some suggestions for creating questions that target individual faculty needs and interests.

In the final article, Jennifer Franklin provides information about how faculty can use the data on their own student ratings to develop a narrative that will help others (such as administrators and the public) understand what the numbers mean and how they should and should not be used. These narratives could deepen everyone's understanding of the complexities of teaching and make the evaluation of teaching a learning process in itself.

Karron G. Lewis
Editor

KARRON G. LEWIS *is the associate director of the Center for Teaching Effectiveness at the University of Texas at Austin.*

1

*When student ratings are mentioned, the discussion often
turns emotional. The abundance of research on these
feedback mechanisms, however, can show how to use
them to learn how to make teaching more effective and
student learning longer lasting.*

Faculty Thoughts and Concerns About Student Ratings

John C. Ory

"Hey, doesn't your office administer the student ratings on campus?"

And so begins another opportunity to listen to faculty concerns about
student ratings of instruction, dispel popular myths, and try to explain how
we prefer rating forms to be administered and the results used on campus.
The collection of student ratings of instruction to evaluate faculty and
courses has become commonplace at most universities, with some high
stakes (Seldin, 1999). It is only natural for faculty to be curious and concerned about the student rating process.

Unfortunately, there are probably more misconceptions about student
ratings than facts known about them, yet we do know quite a bit. Cashin
stated as long ago as 1988 that there were over thirteen hundred articles and
books dealing with research on student ratings. So what do we know? Sit
back, grab a cup of coffee, and read on as I let you listen in on a conversation that I have at least once a month with faculty who have cornered me
on the bus, at a football game, or in the grocery store. It is a conversation
about the knowns and unknowns of student ratings.

The day began as most other days do: I was standing in line holding the
door outside the espresso café when I first heard it.

"It's just a big personality contest and you know it!"

I immediately knew what the conversation was all about. Three professors standing in line ahead of me were discussing what our office had
just delivered the day before: student rating results for the fall semester. I
quickly sized up the threesome before they spotted me. The two men were
a much-experienced full professor in chemistry and a recently hired assistant

NEW DIRECTIONS FOR TEACHING AND LEARNING, no. 87, Fall 2001 © John Wiley & Sons, Inc.

professor in history. The woman was an associate professor in engineering. Did I really want to be a part of this conversation so early in the morning? Maybe I can go without coffee today. Too late. Bill, the chemistry professor, spots me:

BILL: Hey, John, you can appreciate this. I was just trying to tell my younger colleagues here how much students want a show these days; they want to be entertained. Your office's ratings prove this, right?

ME: Well, I can't really agree with you, Bill. I know that many professors believe that good entertainers receive higher ratings than do less flashy but better instructors. However, my office really supports the phrase, "hardness of head and softness of heart" [Goldsmid, Gruber, and Wilson, 1977], to summarize how students define excellence in teaching. Students want instructors who know what they are talking about and who also care about them. As I have said many times before, neither the stand-up comic with no content expertise nor the cold-fish expert with only content expertise receives the highest ratings consistently.

Sometimes I wish I could bottle a sense of humor and sell it to a few of our instructors. Everyone appreciates a good storyteller or a charismatic speaker, but the research has shown that if instructors' personality traits affect their students, it may be caused more by what they do in their teaching than by who they are [Erdle, Murray, and Rushton, 1985]. The influence of the personality of a teacher is important but has not been seen to invalidate or bias student ratings as one piece of evidence in assessing teaching effectiveness.

BILL: I'm not sure I really buy that, but I will give you the benefit of the doubt. So tell me this: Why are the ratings for my two courses so different?

ME: Let me answer that question by asking a couple more. First, are students required to take both courses, or are they taken as electives? Research has shown that ratings in elective courses are higher than in required courses [Costin, Greenough, and Menges, 1971; Feldman, 1978; McKeachie, 1979; Marsh, 1984]. Research on our own campus ratings [Brandenburg, Slinde, and Batista, 1977] has led us to create separate norms for courses that are taken as electives, mixed elective and required, and required. It is the one variable that we believe is consistent and strong enough to be controlled for in our reporting. There are other factors that may influence ratings—I will mention some in a moment—but none that we believe has a significant impact.

Let me also ask whether both of your courses are taught at the same level. Research has shown that ratings in higher-level courses tend to be higher than in lower-level courses [Aleamoni and Graham, 1974; Bausell and Bausell, 1979; Feldman, 1978; Kulik and McKeachie, 1975]. But again, remember that the influence of course level on student ratings is reported to be marginal.

JIM: What about class size? I teach very large classes in history. Certainly class size must affect my ratings!

ME: Let me be honest, and say I believe I can get higher ratings teaching a class of 20 than I can teaching a class of 250. But do you know what? The research doesn't support my belief. In his review of fifty-two studies of student ratings collected in classes of different sizes, Feldman [1978] found an average correlation of $-.09$ between class size and various student rating items. In 1992, Cashin concluded, "Taken alone, class size is not a serious source of bias" [p. 2], and a year later, Centra wrote that rating differences due to class size "have little practical significance" [1993b, p. 102].

But just to show you how stubborn we are in our office, we tried one more time to study the relationship between class size and student ratings. A recent student dissertation [Chiu, 1999] used an unbalanced nested ANOVA design to study the relationship of class size and student ratings. Chiu determined that class size accounted for less than 1 percent of variance in the ratings. I think my office is finally ready to put the issue of class size to rest.

BILL: Okay, if you won't let Jim use class size as an excuse for low ratings, what about the fact that I teach in the hard sciences? Isn't it a fact that courses in the sciences receive lower ratings than do courses in the fine arts or humanities?

ME: Well, Bill, you raise a very timely question. If our office is tempted to do anything different in the way we process and report student ratings, it is in the area of reporting separate norms for different disciplines. Recent research is convincing us that instructors teaching in certain disciplines receive higher student ratings than instructors in other disciplines [Cashin, 1990, 1992; Centra, 1993b; Franklin and Theall, 1992]. In descending order, the disciplines are arts and humanities, biological and social sciences, business, computer science, math, engineering, and physical science. These reported discipline differences are not large, but they are consistent.

What are we going to do? We're not sure. The dissertation that I spoke about earlier [Chiu, 1999] also looked at discipline differences. Discipline accounted for only 1.19 percent of the rating variance. Although this is not very significant, the fact remains that we continue to account for the student motivation variable—that is, required versus elective—which accounts for only 1.29 percent of the variance. Either we stop accounting for the motivation variable, due to its minimal influence, or begin accounting for discipline, seeing that it was the only other variable accounting for more than 1 percent. How would the three of you like to be on a faculty committee to help us decide what to do?

SUE: I don't know about being on another committee, but I would really like someone to consider my situation. My female colleagues keep trying to convince me that in general, women receive lower ratings than do men. Is this true?

ME: Not really. Research again shows no significant relationship between gender of instructor and his or her overall evaluation [Bennett, 1982: Ferber and Huber, 1975; Lombardo and Tocci, 1979; Strathan, Richardson, and Cook, 1991; Wilson and Doyle, 1976]. In his review of gender and rating studies, Feldman [1993] found a correlation of .02 between gender and overall evaluations, with female instructors receiving slightly higher ratings. However, there is some evidence to suggest that ratings are slightly higher in classes in which most students are of the same gender as the instructor. Sue, this may be of most interest to you being in the college of engineering, where there are still many more male than female students. Yet, again, the differences reported are marginal.

As long as we are talking about instructor characteristics, let me say that rank, age, years of experience, and research productivity all have minimal impact on student ratings. We know that professors receive higher ratings than do teaching assistants [Brandenburg, Slinde, and Batista, 1977; Centra and Creech, 1976], and first-year professors usually receive lower ratings than do experienced instructors [Feldman, 1983]. Some studies indicate that faculty research productivity is positively related to their student ratings of effectiveness [Feldman, 1987], and others report a zero correlation between productivity and ratings [Hattie and Marsh, 1996]. As for the race of the instructor, we have yet to see evidence of a biasing impact on ratings.

JIM: You are slowly convincing me there isn't much relationship between instructor characteristics and student ratings, but what about student characteristics?

ME: Remember, I am not trying to convince you of anything. I am merely trying to point out things we think we know about student ratings based on years of research. As John Centra wrote in his book Reflective Faculty Evaluation, "The research on student evaluations, like that on other teacher-evaluation methods, shows significant tendencies but no certainties" [1993b, p. 51].

So let's talk about student characteristics. Once again, there are some consistent trends but each of little consequence. Similar to elective courses, students with prior interest in a course give somewhat higher ratings [Marsh and Cooper, 1981; Ory, 1980; Perry, Abrami, Leventhal, and Check, 1979]. Majors tend to rate instructors more positively than nonmajors [Feldman, 1978]. As I mentioned before when talking about the gender of the instructor, the gender of students is not related to his or her responses, although students tend to rate same-sex instructors slightly higher [Basow and Silberg, 1987; Bennett, 1982; Bernard, Keefauver, Elsworth, and Maylor, 1981;

Feldman, 1992]. And there appears to be no meaningful and consistent relationships between personality characteristics of the students and their ratings [Abrami, Perry, and Leventhal, 1982].

There is one particular student characteristic that deserves special consideration. The research consistently shows that students expecting high grades in a course give higher ratings than do students expecting low grades [Abrami, Dickens, Perry, and Leventhal, 1980; Feldman, 1976; Howard and Maxwell, 1980; Marsh, 1987]. Research on our campus rating system [Instructor and Course Evaluation System] has consistently found a correlation of approximately .30 between expected grade and overall ratings of the instructor and the course. What can we make of this relationship?

Some professors are convinced the relationship proves that easier graders get rewarded for their generosity, regardless of how well they taught [Greenwald and Gillmore, 1997]. Although there may be some truth to that interpretation, I offer another plausible explanation. Students who feel they have learned a lot expect high grades for their efforts and in turn rate their instructors high for good teaching. I am certain the "true" explanation for the relationship involves some of both interpretations. Regardless, several researchers have described the relationship between expected grade and ratings to be minimal [Howard and Maxwell, 1980], "relatively unimportant when ratings are used to make gross distinctions between teachers" [Abrami, Dickens, Perry, and Leventhal, 1980, p. 107], and "relatively small and inconsistent" [Centra, 1993b, p. 74].

SUE: I guess you are trying to tell us that it may not be whom we are or whom we teach but what we do in the classroom that really matters.

ME: For the most part. Certainly all of the factors and variables that you are asking about account for some of the rating variance. But the truth is that professors cannot manipulate the ratings as much as they think they can.

SUE: I may not be able to raise my ratings artificially, but I can certainly tell you how to lower them. Just give the ratings right after your final exam! That will lower them.

ME: You're right. Ratings administered during a final exam are generally lower than those given during a regular class period [Frey, 1976]. Yet how we go about administering ratings in our classes doesn't always have a negative impact. For example, signed ratings are more positive than anonymous ratings [Argulewiz and O'Keefe, 1978; Feldman, 1979; Hartnett and Seligsohn, 1967; Stone, Spool, and Rabinowitz, 1977]. Ratings are more positive if the stated use is for promotion [Centra, 1976; Feldman, 1979; Overall and Marsh, 1979]. You can raise the ratings even a little higher if you stay in the room during administration [Feldman, 1979] or have an administrator hand out the forms following a short speech about their importance [Frey, 1976].

Fortunately, the manner in which you administer ratings has only marginal impact on your ratings. As with everything else we have discussed, manipulating your administration procedures will not turn your ratings from mediocre to excellent. We do wish everyone would follow our recommended administration procedures to keep the playing field as level as possible. There are some excellent resources on how to administer and report student ratings available if you are interested [Cashin, 1999; Theall and Franklin, 1990].

BILL: Obviously, you really believe collecting student ratings is the best method for evaluating teaching.

ME: I am so glad you said that! It really concerns me when I find units on campus overemphasizing the importance of student ratings or relying solely on their use for evaluating teaching. The collection of student ratings is not the only way or the best way but rather one way to evaluate instruction. Our office, as well as other professionals in the field [Braskamp and Ory, 1994; Centra, 1993a; Doyle, 1983; Seldin, 1999], have advocated a multiple-source and multiple-method approach to evaluating teaching effectiveness. The collection of student ratings should be combined with data collected from different sources using various methods, such as peer reviews, teaching portfolios, classroom observations, or self-evaluations.

I am not saying that student ratings are not reliable and valid measures of teaching effectiveness. They are. The reliability of student ratings, or the agreement among student raters within a class [consistency] and the agreement among raters assessing the same instructor at different times [stability] is supported by the results of numerous studies [Feldman, 1977; Murray, Rushton, and Paunonen, 1990].

As for validity, I believe the validity of student ratings is best summarized by Anthony Greenwald [1997] when he wrote, "The validity of student rating measures of instructional quality was severely questioned in the 1970s. By the early 1980s, however, most expert opinion viewed student ratings as valid and as worthy of widespread use" [p. 1182].

BILL: How has the validity of ratings been proven?

ME: Essentially, there have been five types of research studies conducted: multisection, multitrait-multimethod, bias, laboratory designs, and dimensionality. This is probably more detail than you want, but let me briefly describe the different study types. The first study type, multisection, is used to assess the relationship between student ratings and student achievement in multiple sections of the same course taught by different instructors. Researchers correlate the section mean student ratings with the section mean student achievement scores on a common examination. Overall, multisection validity studies have shown substantial correlations with student achievement as measured by examination performance [Abrami, d'Apollonia, and Cohen, 1990; d'Apollonia and Abrami, 1997].

In multitrait-multimethod studies, researchers assess the convergent and discriminant validity of student ratings by correlating them with selected criterion measures of effective instruction, such as alumni ratings, peer ratings, and self-ratings, across a variety of courses. These studies attempt to attribute class-mean differences in ratings and criterion measures to instructors and not to extraneous characteristics such as students, the course, and setting variables. A typical multitrait-multimethod study examines assessments collected from different sources—say, peers, students, alumni, and self-using different methods—for example, open- and closed-ended rating items and interviews. Results have generally shown evidence for both convergent and discriminant validity [Howard, Conway, and Maxwell, 1985; Marsh, 1982].

In general, the research [source: adapted with permission from *Evaluating Teaching Effectiveness* by Braskamp, L. A., Brandenburg, D. C., and Ory, J. C. Newbury Park, Calif.: Sage, 1984, p. 47] shows:

- High positive correlations between student and alumni ratings of instructor effectiveness [Howard, Conway, and Maxwell, 1985; Marsh, 1977; Overall and Marsh, 1980]
- Moderate positive correlations between student and colleague ratings of instructor effectiveness [Feldman, 1989] and between student achievement and student ratings of instructor effectiveness [Cohen, 1981]
- Low positive correlations between student and faculty self-ratings of instructor effectiveness [Blackburn and Clark, 1975; Braskamp, Caulley, and Costin, 1979], between student and administrator ratings of instructor effectiveness [Feldman, 1989], and between student rating of instructor and peer ratings of portfolios [Centra, 1993a]

We have already talked about the third type of research. Bias studies attempt to identify extraneous influences on student ratings, such as those we have already talked about. As I said earlier, the many factors studied have relatively small effects [McKeachie, 1979] and can be controlled or accounted for by the users of student ratings.

The fourth type of validity studies are laboratory studies that examine the relationship between student ratings and experimenter-controlled variables in nonnaturalistic settings, such as videotaped lessons and lab-delivered lectures. For example, different videotaped lectures may be presented to a group of student volunteers who are told different stories regarding the expertise of the lecturer. Due to the laboratory or artificial nature of these studies, their evidence has been viewed as inconclusive regarding the validity of student ratings.

The fifth type of validity attempts to identify the conceptual structure of ratings. Many studies [Feldman, 1976; Kulik and McKeachie, 1975;

Marsh, 1987] have been conducted, reviewed, or meta-analyzed attempting to identify a common set of factors underlying the construct being measured by student ratings of instruction. Although there is some consistency across studies, results fail to identify a single set of dimensions and merely support the notion that students view instructional quality as multidimensional.

If you want to know more about the validity of student ratings, I can recommend a couple of good articles [Abrami, d'Apollonia, and Cohen, 1990; Ory and Ryan, 2001].

SUE: All that research sounds impressive, but how valid is the rating process if it makes my colleagues teach to the ratings—that is, change their teaching to address the item content on the rating forms?

ME: I believe you are addressing a rather recent concern about student ratings: What are the consequences of their use? With so many colleges and universities reporting the use of student ratings in personnel decisions, the consequences of their use and interpretations need to be addressed, including both negative and positive consequences and intended and unintended consequences. It is certainly time to consider the consequential basis for the validity of student ratings [McKeachie, 1997].

I just happen to have in my briefcase a listing of possible consequences, both intended and unintended, of using student ratings that a colleague and I included in a recent publication [Ory and Ryan, 2001, p. 39].

Intended
- Instructors collect ratings, value the input, and make improvements in their teaching and courses.
- Instructors are rewarded for having excellent rating results (e.g., salary, promotion, awards, recognition).
- Instructors with very low ratings are encouraged by their department to seek help, possibly from colleagues or a campus faculty development office.
- Students perceive and use ratings as a means for indicating suggestions for improvement.
- Students have more information on which to base their course selections.
- Instructors use ratings as motivation to improve their teaching.
- Students perceive ratings as a vehicle for change.

Unintended
- Instructors alter their teaching in order to receive high ratings (lower content difficulty, provide less content, give only high grades).
- The campus rewards poor teaching (lower faculty standards).
- Due to their convenience, the campus looks to student ratings as the only measure of teaching quality.
- The content of the student rating form may determine what is addressed in the classroom.

- Students reward poor teaching by believing they can give high ratings in return for high grades.
- Ratings are used to make discriminations between instructors that cannot be supported by the data.
- Due to the high stakes involved, instructors fail to follow proper administration procedures.
- The rating process becomes a meaningless activity that is only performed by students and instructors because it is mandated.

How often or to what extent do these consequences take place? Are they potential or actual problems at our institution? We need to find the answers to these questions by doing more to understand the ratings process and its consequences. It's somewhat similar to the use of a standardized test. We may have evidence that an exam covers the appropriate content at a desired level of difficulty. However, if we find teachers teaching to the test or the exam being used for unintended purposes, both consequences would invalidate our interpretation of the test scores.

Now let me address your concern more directly. It's good to hear stories of faculty changing their teaching after receiving ratings results. After all, our goal is to improve instruction. Furthermore, I don't mind it if an instructor tells me, "If all I have to do is offer more office hours to get higher student ratings, then I'll do it." I won't question the motives if the change addresses student concerns. What I am concerned about is when a faculty member looks at the student rating form content as a set of desired teaching behaviors and tries to change his or her teaching style accordingly. If use of student ratings is seen to reinforce specific teaching behaviors, their use may constrict rather than encourage a diversity of classroom strategies. This would be what I have called a negative consequence of student ratings.

BILL: Exactly! So what can we do about it?

ME: To improve the validity of our student ratings, we need both to improve our practices and conduct research on their use and consequences. There are five major users of student ratings on campus: campus evaluation offices, campus committees, administrators, faculty, and students. Each group can improve its use of student ratings and possibly avoid negative consequences. For example, administrators and campus committees must avoid using ratings as the only evidence of teaching quality. Faculty need to know of and follow proper administration procedures. Students must act responsibly in their rating of faculty. Finally, evaluation offices like my own should conduct research to determine the existence of intended and unintended consequences, as well as to inform faculty of the research on student rating research. Your questions make me realize how much more offices like mine need to do to keep you and all other users of student ratings informed of what, why, and how we do what we do. Anything else?

JIM: So what did you say was the secret to getting high ratings? Just kidding! Despite our concerns and some skepticism about student ratings, I would imagine that we have all changed, and I hope improved, our teaching by reading our rating results, especially the students' comments on the back of the form. They can be frustrating, but they are often very useful.

ME: Student ratings are not perfect measures that can be easily misused. Yet I have always believed the students are our consumers, and unless they have not been attending class, as consumers they have a legitimate voice to be heard. Now I personally believe we shouldn't ask them about things they can't evaluate, such as the content of the course. How do they know if the material is current or out of date? They can, however, comment on whether they are getting ample amounts of feedback on tests, getting their assignments back, or learning much in the course.

Let me end by saying how pleased I am to hear that you have made changes in your teaching based on the ratings. Do you ever share those changes with the students? I mean, do you ever start a new semester by explaining to the new students some changes you made based on the ratings from the previous semester? Students are often frustrated when they think that their opinions don't matter, and faculty are concerned that students don't take the rating process seriously. Just by dropping a comment or two about your use of ratings, I believe you can help us address both concerns.

I am sure you didn't expect all of this with your opening question! If you want to know more about evaluating your teaching, stop by my office; I can lend you a few useful books on the topic [Centra, 1993b; Seldin, 1999; Braskamp and Ory, 1994].

CASHIER: That will be $1.85, please.

BILL, SUE, JIM: [In unison] We'll get that for you, John. We appreciated your time this morning. Plus, we assume you purposefully left out our ability to raise student ratings through good old-fashioned bribery. Right?

References

Abrami, P. C., d'Apollonia, S., and Cohen, P. A. "The Validity of Student Ratings of Instruction: What We Know and What We Don't." *Journal of Educational Psychology,* 1990, *82,* 219–231.

Abrami, P. C., Dickens, W. J., Perry, R. P., and Leventhal, L. "Do Teacher Standards for Assigning Grades Affect Student Evaluations of Teaching?" *Journal of Educational Psychology,* 1980, *72,* 107–118.

Abrami, P. C., Perry, R. P., and Leventhal, L. "The Relationship Between Student Personality Characteristics, Teacher Ratings, and Student Achievement." *Journal of Educational Psychology,* 1982, *74,* 111–125.

Aleamoni, L. M., and Graham, N. H. "The Relationship Between CEQ Ratings and Instructor's Rank, Class Size, and Course Level." *Journal of Educational Measurement,* 1974, *11,* 189–201.

Argulewiz, E., and O'Keefe, T. "An Investigation of Signed Versus Anonymously Completed Ratings of High School Student Teachers." *Educational Research Journal*, 1978, *3*, 39–44.

Basow, S. A., and Silberg, N. T. "Student Evaluations of College Professors: Are Female and Male Professors Rated Differently?" *Journal of Educational Psychology*, 1987, *79*, 308–314.

Bausell, R. B., and Bausell, C. R. "Student Ratings and Various Instructional Variables from a Within-Instructor Perspective." *Research in Higher Education*, 1979, *11*, 167–177.

Bennett, S. K. "Student Perceptions of and Expectations for Male and Female Instructors: Evidence Relating to the Question of Gender Bias in Teaching Evaluation." *Journal of Educational Psychology*, 1982, *74*, 170–179.

Bernard, M. E., Keefauver, L. W., Elsworth, G., and Maylor, F. D. "Sex Role Behavior and Gender in Teacher-Student Evaluations." *Journal of Educational Psychology*, 1981, *73*, 681–696.

Blackburn, R. T., and Clark, M. J. "An Assessment of Faculty Performance: Some Correlates Between Administrators, Colleagues, Student, and Self-Ratings." *Sociology of Education*, 1975, *48*, 242–256.

Brandenburg, D. C., Slinde, J. A., and Batista, E. E. "Student Ratings of Instruction: Validity and Normative Interpretations." *Journal of Research in Higher Education*, 1977, *7*, 67–68.

Braskamp, L. A., Brandenburg, D. C., and Ory, J. C. *Evaluating Teaching Effectiveness: A Practical Guide*. Thousand Oaks, Calif.: Sage, 1984.

Braskamp, L. A., Caulley, D. N., and Costin, F. "Student Ratings and Instructor Self-Ratings and Their Relationship to Student Achievement." *American Educational Research Journal*, 1979, *16*, 295–306.

Braskamp, L. A., and Ory, J. C. *Assessing Faculty Work*. San Francisco: Jossey-Bass, 1994.

Cashin, W. E. *Student Ratings of Teaching: A Summary of the Research*. Manhattan: Center for Faculty Evaluation and Development, Kansas State University, 1988.

Cashin, W. E. "Students Do Rate Different Academic Fields Differently." In M. Theall and J. Franklin (eds.), *Student Ratings of Instruction: Issues for Improving Practice*. New Directions for Teaching and Learning, no. 43. San Francisco: Jossey-Bass, 1990.

Cashin, W. E. "Student Ratings: The Need for Comparative Data." *Instructional Evaluation and Faculty Development*, 1992, *12*, 1–6.

Cashin, W. E. "Student Ratings of Teaching: Uses and Misuses." In Peter Seldin (ed.), *Changing Practices in Evaluating Teaching*. Bolton, Mass.: Anker, 1999.

Centra, J. A. "The Influence of Different Directions on Student Ratings of Instruction." *Journal of Educational Measurement*, 1976, *13*, 277–282.

Centra, J. A. "Use of the Teaching Portfolio and Student Evaluations for Summative Evaluation." Paper presented at the annual meeting of the American Educational Research Association, Atlanta, Apr. 1993a.

Centra, J. A. *Reflective Faculty Evaluation*. San Francisco: Jossey-Bass, 1993b.

Centra, J. A., and Creech, F. R. *The Relationship Between Students, Teachers, and Course Characteristics and Student Ratings of Teacher Effectiveness*. Princeton, N.J.: Educational Testing Service, 1976.

Chiu, S. "Use of the Unbalanced Nested ANOVA to Exam Factors Influencing Student Ratings of Instructional Quality." Unpublished doctoral dissertation, University of Illinois at Urbana-Champaign, 1999.

Cohen, P. A. "Student Ratings of Instruction and Student Achievement: A Meta-Analysis of Multisection Validity Studies." *Review of Educational Research*, 1981, *51*, 281–309.

Costin, F., Greenough, W. T., and Menges, R. J. "Student Ratings of College Teaching: Reliability, Validity, and Usefulness." *Review of Educational Research*, 1971, *41*, 511–535.

d'Apollonia, S., and Abrami, P. C. "Navigating Student Ratings of Instruction." *American Psychologist*, 1997, *52*, 1198–1208.

Doyle, K. O. *Evaluating Teaching*. San Francisco: New Lexington Press, 1983.

Erdle, S., Murray, H. G., and Rushton, J. P. "Personality, classroom, behavior, and college teaching effectiveness: A path analysis." *Journal of Educational Psychology*, 1985, *77*, 394–407.

Feldman, K. A. "Grades and College Students' Evaluations of Their Courses and Teachers." *Research in Higher Education,* 1976, *4,* 69–111.

Feldman, K. A. "Consistency and Variability Among College Students in Rating Their Teachers and Courses: A Review and Analysis." *Research in Higher Education,* 1977, *6,* 223–274.

Feldman, K. A. "Course Characteristics and College Students' Ratings of Their Teachers and Courses: What We Know and What We Don't." *Research in Higher Education,* 1978, *9,* 199–242.

Feldman, K. A. "The Significance of Circumstances for College Students' Ratings of Their Teachers and Courses: A Review and Analysis." *Research in Higher Education,* 1979, *10,* 149–172.

Feldman, K. A. "Seniority and Experience of College Teachers as Related to Evaluations They Receive from Their Students." *Research in Higher Education,* 1983, *18,* 3–124.

Feldman, K. A. "Research Productivity and Scholarly Accomplishments of College Teachers as Related to Their Institutional Effectiveness: A Review and Exploration." *Research in Higher Education,* 1987, *26,* 227–291.

Feldman, K. A. "The Association Between Student Ratings of Specific Instructional Dimensions and Student Achievement: Refining and Extending the Synthesis of Data from Multisection Validity Studies." *Research in Higher Education,* 1989, *30,* 583–645.

Feldman, K. A. "College Students' Views of Male and Female College Teachers: Part I— Evidence from the Social Laboratory and Experiments." *Research in Higher Education,* 1992, *33,* 317–375.

Feldman, K. A. "College Students' Views of Male and Female College Teachers: Part II— Evidence from Students' Evaluations of Their Classroom Teachers." *Research in Higher Education,* 1993, *34,* 151–211.

Ferber, M. A., and Huber, J. A. "Sex of Student and Instructor: A Study of Student Bias." *American Journal of Sociology,* 1975, *80,* 949–963.

Franklin, J., and Theall, M. "Disciplinary Differences: Instructional Goals and Activities, Measures of Student Performance, and Student Ratings of Instruction." Paper presented at the annual meeting of the American Educational Research Association, Boston, Apr. 1992.

Frey, P. W. "Validity of Student Instructional Ratings as a Function of Their Timing." *Journal of Higher Education,* 1976, *47,* 327–336.

Goldsmid, C. A., Gruber, M. E., and Wilson, E. K. "Perceived Attributes of Superior Teachers (PAST): An Inquiry into the Giving of Teaching Awards." *American Educational Research Journal,* 1977, *14,* 423–440.

Greenwald, A. G. "Validity Concerns and Usefulness of Student Ratings of Instruction." *American Psychologist,* 1997, *52,* 1182–1186.

Greenwald, A. G., and Gillmore, G. M. "Grading Leniency Is a Removable Contaminant of Student Ratings." *American Psychologist,* 1997, *52,* 1209–1217.

Hartnett, R. T., and Seligsohn, H. C. "The Effects of Varying Degrees of Anonymity on Responses to Different Types of Psychological Questionnaires." *Journal of Educational Measurement,* 1967, *4,* 95–103.

Hattie, J., and Marsh, H. W. "The Relationship Between Research and Teaching: A Meta-Analysis." *Review of Educational Research,* 1996, *66,* 507–542.

Howard, G. S., Conway, C. G., and Maxwell, S. E. "Construct Validity of Measures of College Teaching Effectiveness." *Journal of Educational Psychology,* 1985, *77,* 187–196.

Howard, G. S., and Maxwell, S. E. "Correlation Between Student Satisfaction and Grades: A Case of Mistaken Causation?" *Journal of Educational Psychology,* 1980, *72,* 810–820.

Kulik, J. A., and McKeachie, W. J. "The Evaluation of Teachers in Higher Education." In F. N. Kerlinger (ed.), *Review of Research in Education.* Itasca, Ill.: Peacock, 1975.

Lombardo, J., and Tocci, M. E. "Attribution of Positive and Negative Characteristics of Instructors." *Perceptual and Motor Skills,* 1979, *48,* 491–494.

Marsh, H. W. "The Validity of Students' Evaluations: Classroom Evaluations of Instructors Independently Nominated as Best or Worst Teachers by Graduating Seniors." *American Educational Research Journal,* 1977, *14,* 441–447.

Marsh, H. W. "Validity of Students' Evaluations of College Teaching: A Multitrait-Multimethod Analysis." *Journal of Educational Psychology,* 1982, *74,* 264–279.

Marsh, H. W. "Students' Evaluation of University Teaching: Dimensionality, Reliability, Validity, Potential Biases, and Utility." *Journal of Educational Psychology,* 1984, *76,* 707–754.

Marsh, H. W. "Students' Evaluations of University Teaching: Research Findings, Methodological Issues, and Directions for Future Research." *International Journal of Educational Research,* 1987, *11,* 253–388.

Marsh, H. W., and Cooper, T. "Prior Subject Interest, Students' Evaluation, and Instructional Effectiveness." *Multivariate Behavioral Research,* 1981, *16,* 82–104.

McKeachie, W. J. "Student Ratings of Faculty: A Reprise." *Academe,* 1979, *65,* 384–397.

McKeachie, W. J. "Student Ratings: The Validity of Use." *American Psychologist,* 1997, *52,* 1218–1225.

Murray, H. G., Rushton, J. P., and Paunonen, S. V. "Teacher Personality Traits and Student Instructional Ratings in Six Types of University Courses." *Journal of Educational Psychology,* 1990, *82,* 250–261.

Ory, J. C. "The Influence of Students' Affective Entry on Instructor and Course Evaluations." *Review of Higher Education,* 1980, *4,* 13–24.

Ory, J. C., and Ryan, K. "How do student ratings measure up to a new validity framework?" In M. Theall, P. Abrami, and L. Mets (eds.), *The student ratings debate: Are they valid? How can we best use them?* New Directions for Institutional Research, no. 109, San Francisco: Jossey-Bass, 2001.

Overall, J. U., and Marsh, H. W. "Midterm Feedback from Students: Its Relationship to Instructional Improvement and Students' Cognitive and Affective Outcomes." *Journal of Educational Psychology,* 1979, *71,* 856–865.

Overall, J. U., and Marsh, H. W. "Students' Evaluations of Instruction: A Longitudinal Study of Their Stability." *Journal of Educational Psychology,* 1980, *72,* 321–325.

Perry, R. P., Abrami, P. C., Leventhal, L., and Check, J. "Instructor Reputation: An Expectancy Relationship Involving Student Ratings and Achievement." *Journal of Educational Psychology,* 1979, *71,* 776–787.

Seldin, P. (ed.). *Changing Practices in Evaluating Teaching.* Bolton, Mass.: Anker, 1999.

Stone, E. F., Spool, M. D., and Rabinowitz, S. "Effects of Anonymity and Retaliatory Potential on Student Evaluations of Faculty Performance." *Research in Higher Education,* 1977, *6,* 313–325.

Strathan, A., Richardson, L., and Cook, J. A. *Gender and University Teaching.* Albany: State University of New York Press, 1991.

Theall, M., and Franklin, J. (eds.). *Student Ratings of Instruction: Issues for Improving Practice.* New Directions for Teaching and Learning, no. 43. San Francisco: Jossey-Bass, 1990.

Wilson, D., and Doyle, K. G., Jr. "Student Ratings of Instruction." *Journal of Higher Education,* 1976, *47,* 465–470.

JOHN C. ORY is the director of the Office of Instructional Resources at the University of Illinois at Urbana-Champaign.

2

Giving feedback is a skill that can be learned. What are the conditions that foster that learning and the later use of that skill for feedback to instructors?

Encouraging Your Students to Give Feedback

Marilla D. Svinicki

"This class was great!" "This class was horrible." "The instructor was so disorganized." "The tests were soooo unfair."

Are there any instructors who have received these kinds of vague comments from students and have not wondered, "What does this mean?" Even more frustrating is receiving no comments at all from students, just the results from the typical scaled student evaluation survey. This volume is about what to do with such results, but perhaps the best thing to do would be to improve the quality of student comments and prevent the frustration in the first place. This article provides instructors with the kinds of suggestions that will help them help students be better evaluators of instruction.

In the mid-1980s, my university decided to revamp its student evaluation of the teaching process. At that time, the system consisted of a large number of Likert scale items pointing at different aspects of the course and instructor, and a free-response section where students could write whatever their muse inspired them to write. In good assessment methodology, we polled the various users of the form to identify their needs and their preferences. The faculty who responded gave a resounding endorsement to the written comments from the students in comparison to the scaled items. As a result, we proposed doing away with the scaled items altogether and concentrating on encouraging student written comments, but there were too many individuals at various levels of decision making who would be lost without numbers, so both parts of the survey were retained. The revealing part of this story is the solid preference for student written comments exhibited by those faculty who responded, despite the common confusion that the comments sometimes elicit. This finding has been reported in other

NEW DIRECTIONS FOR TEACHING AND LEARNING, no. 87, Fall 2001   © John Wiley & Sons, Inc.

work (Ory and Braskamp, 1981; Tiberius, Sackin, and Cappe, 1987). Because this is the preferred mode for faculty to receive feedback, it is worthwhile to think about ways of encouraging more and better student comments.

Why Don't Students Give More Feedback?

Although there are many possible reasons for the frequent lack of student open-ended comments, I believe that two general areas account for the bulk of this problem: student beliefs about feedback and their lack of understanding and practice in giving it.

Student Beliefs About Feedback. The general literature on motivation problems says that an individual who believes that his efforts will not result in any change in the situation is less motivated to make any effort. Taken to its extreme, this phenomenon has been referred to as learned helplessness (Peterson, Maier, and Seligman, 1993). One frequent characteristic of someone experiencing learned helplessness is passivity, that is, a failure to respond at all. If we translate that into the problem with student feedback, we might say that students are not inclined to give extensive feedback because they believe it will have no effect on the ultimate target of teaching. Certainly, they have seen enough examples of continuing poor teaching in the face of student evaluation of teaching to make them skeptical about whether anyone actually reads the feedback. Without evidence of attention to this feedback, students could well conclude that the effort necessary to give feedback is not worth putting forth.

In less psychological terms, we could observe that the same experience of no effect can result in cynicism about the process altogether, another posture that institutions do not wish to foster in students. Cynicism is often followed by withdrawal from the process, as seen when students write nothing at all or leave before the evaluation is completed.

Another student belief about giving feedback revolves around the notion of retribution on the part of the instructor. This has been one of the arguments for making the student evaluations anonymous (Gordon and Stuecher, 1992). Students often feel that if they give negative feedback, it will somehow come back to haunt them. These worries make them less likely to provide extensive comments, particularly if those comments are negative and would suggest "better" ways of teaching.

Lack of Understanding or Practice. This second source of problems with student feedback is both attitudinal and practical. Motivation theory again tells us that if someone does not think he or she can successfully accomplish a task, motivation to engage in it falls. In this case, faced with the request for feedback and a lack of a clear understanding about how to give it, students may choose to say nothing at all or make very general statements that could not be criticized.

Indeed, there has been little opportunity for students to learn the skill of giving feedback to teachers. Learning this skill would require some sort of feedback on the feedback, and the typical student evaluation of teaching usually disappears from students' thoughts once it has been completed. Students have no opportunity to see models of good feedback or receive any feedback on whether what they wrote was helpful or useless. The rise of collaborative learning models is starting to make some inroads into teaching students how to respond to the work of others, but it would be a stretch to assume that students could translate those skills into feedback to their instructors.

Improving Student Written Feedback

Learning to give good feedback is much like learning any other skill: it requires motivation, direct teaching, and optimal conditions for practice.

Motivation. The motivation level that students bring to their giving of feedback is an important determinant of the amount of feedback they will give. The learners must believe that what they are doing will make a difference in a class. How can we convince students that giving feedback is worth their time and energy? One easy first strategy rests on the principle of early success: if the students are given an opportunity to provide early feedback and they see that their feedback is acted on in a positive way, that early success signals to them that this particular instructor is serious about feedback and uses what the class has said in modifying the course. All of the work on midsemester evaluations has shown that gathering feedback early in the semester allows an instructor to turn around even very difficult classes.

This early feedback success can have an impact on the students as well. A common feedback strategy is the use of the one-minute paper. At the end of the class, students are asked to spend one minute commenting on what helped them the most to learn the day's target content or what is still confusing to them. Regular use of such questions can cause the students to engage in the class differently. If they are constantly being asked to give examples of good and poor practice in the class, they eventually begin asking themselves on a regular basis what has been good and what has not helped. They become more critical, reflective observers of their own learning, which is the first step toward becoming a self-regulated learner. What teacher would not want a classroom full of highly reflective, engaged, self-regulated students?

That point aside, the original value of this early feedback is encouraging and improving later feedback. Students learn that their feedback to the instructor makes a difference; they do have an effect. This success then changes their belief that nothing they say matters; they have proof it does.

A second source of motivation to provide feedback can come from the instructor. A persuasively delivered monologue on the degree to which the instructor values student input and how he or she has used it can influence student attitudes as well. It is particularly effective to relate the feedback from previous semesters to the changes students have seen in the current semester. In the course of this inspirational narrative, the instructor can even acknowledge the problems that students have had in the past trying to give feedback to other instructors. Communicating expectations about the feedback is often enough to influence the amounts and kinds of information the students think to give.

Direct Teaching of Giving Feedback. Because the skill of giving feedback is becoming a more and more important one as we move toward teamwork in classes as well as the workplace, one possible solution to the problem of desultory student feedback is to take the time in class to teach students how to give feedback.

According to the literature on learning, one of the best ways to learn a skill (and giving feedback is a skill) is to observe a model (Bandura, 1986). It is likely that students have not seen many good models of feedback for improvement, so one solid instructional strategy would be to provide good models of giving feedback. For example, when giving feedback to students on their own work, an instructor can follow the same guidelines that he or she wants the students to follow in any other feedback situation. No definitive list of guidelines that cuts across all fields stands out, but some of the qualities of effective feedback are frequently mentioned:

• Feedback should be specific, using examples familiar to the individual to make the point. For example, feedback on a student's writing should not simply say something vague like, "Good logic," but instead should point out the characteristics of the writing that contribute to the logic, such as, "A good hierarchical structure of the main points with nice examples and supporting citations for each level; also a good use of relational phrases as transitions between points, which makes the meaning and structure much clearer." Given this level of feedback, a student who was looking to rewrite his paper would have some clear guidelines to follow in the revision process.

The same would hold true for teaching feedback. Rather than saying that the instructor was "so disorganized," students can learn to enumerate the observations that led to such a label—for example, "The instructor frequently forgets where he is in the logic of the lecture and has to retrace his steps, which wastes everyone's time," or "On two occasions, the instructor brought the wrong notes to class for the topic listed on the syllabus."

• Feedback should concentrate on observable behavior rather than inferring what the individual is thinking or feeling. For example, it would be counterproductive to say, "Jim doesn't get his work done because he is irresponsible." It is sufficient simply to observe that his work is not being done and to give a few examples to support that observation. In the same way, student feedback should not make inferences about the instructor's level of caring, because that is not directly observable. Students should instead point out the behaviors that the instructor engages in that make them feel that he does not care. For example, it is much more helpful to say, "I visited his office during office hours at least three times, and he was not there for any of them."

• Feedback should avoid personalization or emotionally charged wording ("This instructor is worthless" or "This instructor doesn't like students"). Sticking to descriptions of actual incidents is much more helpful as feedback.

• Feedback should describe the effect the behavior has on the giver so that the receiver can experience it from a different perspective ("When the instructor uses jargon that we don't know yet, I have trouble taking good notes because I don't understand the words enough to write them down accurately"). Feedback of this type often points toward a solution. In this example, the instructor could stop after the use of jargon and clarify its meaning or give the students time to pause and write it down without breaking the information flow.

• Feedback should offer alternatives to the behavior being criticized. In the previous example, the student might append to that description, "If you could write the technical terms on the board beforehand, I could check my spelling against yours to be sure I had written the words down correctly."

• Feedback should point out good and bad aspects of the instruction. Sprinkling a little praise or understanding throughout feedback helps a receiver be less defensive about negative comments. For example, a student could say, "Although the students who have had more than one prerequisite course probably get a lot out of the more complex examples that you use, I have had a problem understanding the main point because I can't see a good connection. Maybe you could invite us to try to summarize the key ideas, and then go over them briefly to be sure everyone is on the same page."

If the instructor provided that level of feedback to students on their work, it would be an excellent model for their providing feedback too. Spending class time in going over these qualities before asking the students to do any critical feedback, either of the instructor or their peers, would be worthwhile.

Another possibility for modeling can come in peer feedback groups, particularly those associated with editing. When students are asked to give one another feedback, they often find themselves facing the same dilemmas as in giving feedback to instructors: they do not know how to be helpful or want to avoid being perceived as too critical. As a result, they often end up with bland feedback that neither offends nor assists the author. A little time spent as a group in constructing feedback norms or expectations can give the students more confidence in their own ability to handle the situation effectively.

Because we are trying to teach the students to give better feedback, we should not wait until the end of the semester to institute the process. It would be most beneficial to schedule periodic feedback sessions early in the semester. For example, after about the first third of the course or around a critical initial assessment like the first test, conducting a teaching feedback session would make a lot of sense.

The instructor would discuss the rationale for asking for feedback so that the students understood why they were being asked for input and what the possible consequences might be. He or she would also describe the characteristics of good feedback, as outlined in this article, and show some examples of student comments that followed the guidelines. In the initial session, the instructor might make the task a little easier by giving specific prompts to guide student thinking. In later sessions, those prompts could be removed as the students learned the kinds of comments that are the most useful.

Students might work initially in groups to create a set of feedback comments. This would have the benefit of peer modeling as well as alleviating some of the anxiety associated with being the sole evaluator.

Once feedback has been received, it is important for the instructor to respond in a positive way with his or her own reactions, both responding to the specific comments and suggestions made and commenting on the characteristics of the feedback that were most helpful. This would then help shape the students' feedback-giving skills, as well as increase their motivation to respond again next time.

Optimal Conditions for Practice. Once students have learned how to give useful feedback, the instructor needs to establish the conditions under which they can both practice and perform that skill. The practice part of this suggestion simply means that once is not enough; providing students multiple opportunities to practice giving feedback is a necessary supplement to the direct teaching of it. The multiple practice opportunities also provide a good mechanism for an instructor to keep up with students' progress and opinions, an important aspect of responsive teaching.

Perhaps even more important, however, is providing the optimal conditions for giving feedback. There are several ways to improve the conditions under which students give feedback and as a result improve the chances of their providing more thoughtful and useful information. The first of these is giving adequate notice. To elicit carefully considered comments from students requires giving them time beforehand to think about the questions. It is very difficult to come up with coherent, thoughtful feedback with only five minutes' notice. Students will be able to provide much better information if the instructor tells them before class that he or she will be asking for their input at the following session. While it is naive to think that all the students will take the opportunity to ruminate over their responses during that time, it is reasonable to think that enough of them will to make it worthwhile. Certainly, nothing is lost as a result. I have even had students come to the next class period with an essay assessing the various components of the class.

The second way that an instructor can improve the conditions under which feedback is given is to provide adequate instructions, especially the first time: a description of the purpose of the feedback and how it will be handled, how the instructor intends to respond to it, and thanks to the students beforehand. It is also quite useful for the instructor to provide some specific prompts appropriate to the time of the semester. For example, a feedback session early in the semester prior to any exam might have prompts that focus on student understanding of what is being done in class, the nature of the reading assignments, procedural questions, and other things that would indicate that students were adjusting to the flow of the course. A feedback session scheduled on the heels of an exam would have prompts that focused on the difficulty of the exam, what the instructor did that helped or interfered with exam performance, and suggestions for how the instructor could provide more help for the next exam. It would probably also be interesting always to include a prompt that says, "What question should I have asked about the class, and what would your response have been?"

Another condition that might help students give better feedback would be to assign one or more students in the class to be the administrators and summarizers of the feedback. Spence and Lenze discuss this team concept in more detail in their article in this volume. I reinforce it here because of the concern that some students have about retaliation. Having a team of students serve as the go-between should address those concerns. Of course, it is more likely the case that instructors who engage in this kind of ongoing feedback gathering will have a good rapport with the class, such that these concerns are minimized. Nevertheless, the interjection of a third party between the critic and the critiqued can benefit both parties.

A final condition that increases the quality of feedback is providing adequate time for students to think and write. Too often, student feedback is solicited as an afterthought during the last few minutes of the class, when students and instructor are more concerned about getting to their next appointment than doing a thorough job of analyzing the class. Instructors who ask students for their feedback must be sure to give it the time it deserves. Their willingness to take class time to gather feedback makes a statement to the students about its importance. This activity should be treated with the same level of commitment and attention as any other learning activity in the class. And if the instructor has prepared the students and is giving them good prompts to guide their thinking, they should be able to put the time to good use without needing the whole class period.

The Final Step: Be Prepared to Receive the Feedback

Once instructors have high-quality feedback from the students, they must respond to it. Certainly the other articles in this volume provide lots of ways to gather and respond to student feedback. To their suggestions I add my own caution: these efforts will come to naught if the feedback falls on deaf ears or a defensive ego. Teaching is a very personal act, and it is hard to accept criticism of something so close to our essence. But if we cannot or if we react defensively, we destroy all hope of getting honest and useful student feedback from that class again.

I have found that the suggestions discussed in this article decrease the possibility of offensive or useless feedback and increase the quality and instructional value of the comments students will make. We must remember that none of us is so good that we cannot be better.

References

Bandura, A. *Social Foundations of Thought and Action: A Social Cognitive Theory.* Upper Saddle River, N.J.: Prentice Hall, 1986.

Gordon, R. A., and Stuecher, U. "The Effect of Anonymity and Increased Accountability on the Linguistic Complexity of Teaching Evaluations." *Journal of Psychology,* 1992, *126,* 639–650.

Ory, J. C., and Braskamp, L. A. "Faculty Perceptions of the Quality and Usefulness of Three Types of Evaluative Information." *Research in Higher Education,* 1981, *15,* 271–282.

Peterson, C., Maier, S., and Seligman, M. *Learned Helplessness: A Theory for the Age of Personal Control.* New York: Oxford University Press, 1993.

Tiberius, R. G., Sackin, H. D., and Cappe, L. "A Comparison of Two Methods for Evaluating Teaching." *Studies in Higher Education,* 1987, *12,* 287–297.

MARILLA D. SVINICKI is director of the Center for Teaching Effectiveness at the University of Texas at Austin.

3

Most student evaluation instruments include a place for student comments, yet the comments are often difficult to interpret. This article illustrates these comments and uses the information for improving teaching and students' learning.

Making Sense of Student Written Comments

Karron G. Lewis

Probably one of the most difficult tasks for faculty who look at their end-of-semester student evaluations is interpreting what students are saying in their written comments. Invariably, some students say, "You teach the most wonderful class I have ever taken at this university," and others (in the same class) say, "You are such a terrible teacher that you should be fired!"

Many instructors may be tempted to dismiss the important information these comments provide about their teaching and their students' learning because they feel students do not know enough to judge their teaching and "these written comments show just how unreliable they are!" On the other hand, many instructors also say that they get more information from student written comments than they do from the scaled items that are typically found on student evaluation forms. Which is correct? Should we dismiss these student comments or embrace them?

The problem arises from the fact that written comments have no built-in structure like scaled items do. They do not come to the instructor compiled into a neat package that summarizes the positive and negative comments. Instead, they are usually read straight through from the top of the stack to the bottom, so that they seem to be a series of random, unconnected statements about the teaching and the teacher. Under these circumstances, it is difficult for the human mind to make sense of the information. There is a need to impose structure and organization on information in order to make it comprehensible. In other words, we must treat these comments as a set of

---

This article is an adaptation of Lewis, K. G. "Making Sense (and Use) of Written Student Comments." *Teaching Excellence,* 1991, 3.

New Directions for Teaching and Learning, no. 87, Fall 2001 © John Wiley & Sons, Inc.

qualitative data that we need to analyze to make sense of them. This article looks at some ways to impose a little structure on these student comments so that they will make more sense and possibly yield better insights into teaching that might be obscured by a more random presentation of the information.

Qualitative Research Techniques

Qualitative research involves the study of actual situations as they happen naturally, without predetermined constraints on outcomes (Patton, 1990). Philipsen (1982) says that qualitative inquiry is exploratory, openly coded, and participatory. In addition, this type of research seeks to understand the complexity of the whole system under study and recognize that each situation is unique. Wulff and Nyquist (2001) indicate that the primary methods of collecting data for qualitative research are interviewing, observing, and studying printed materials. The student written comments are printed materials and may also be considered a form of interviewing. To analyze the data, we can use conceptual frameworks and matrices. For the purposes of the analysis of student written comments, we will be using a matrix in this article to organize the various ideas expressed by the students.

This discussion of qualitative research techniques and how they pertain to the analysis of student written comments is necessarily very brief. Because teaching environments are complex, each student will probably perceive the teaching and course in a different way. Moreover, individual learning styles can color the way each student reacts to specific environments or teaching strategies. Thus, student comments reflect this complexity. Looking at their comments using qualitative analysis methods can help make sense of what they are saying and provide hints for developing strategies for addressing their concerns.

Getting Started

Making sense of student comments is a multistep process, but it follows a logical course. Most instructors are initially interested in how categories of students perceive the course. Later they find it useful to make further distinctions. Let's consider how you might go about categorizing responses to make them more meaningful.

Sorting by Respondent. Consider the following statements from an engineering course that students generally regard as difficult:

> More lecture would help. More explanation of how to do the problems, not just examples. When exams come, I can usually do the problems assigned or worked in class but the new ones are completely foreign.

> Would rate the course higher if I were understanding material better.

Inability of the instructor to communicate with me during the lecture. He jumps from one thing to another. He is not consistent and he does not finish the job. (To help us understand the whole thing.) In conclusion, his teaching technique is not right.

The only complaint I have is that the exam problems are always more complex than the homework problems and require too much time.

Makes me want to understand the material and making sure I know the concept and mathematical procedures.

The scaled ratings for the same course show how many students selected the following ratings:

One of the Best	2
Above Average	14
Average	5
Below Average	4
Far Below Average	2

From these ratings, one might conclude that the students generally feel the course is all right, but there are a few things that might be changed to make it better. The written comments, on the other hand, certainly indicate some areas of difficulty. How can the instructor sort out this information to make it more helpful and to reconcile the two results?

The first thing that can be done is to group the comments according to the overall course rating given by each student on the evaluation form. This provides a context for the comments, which now read in this order:

- One of the Best (2)
  No comments
- Above Average (14)
  "The only complaint I have is that the exam problems are always more complex than the homework problems and require too much time."
  "Makes me want to understand the material and making sure I know the concept and mathematical procedures."
- Average (5)
  "Would rate the course higher if I were understanding material better."
- Below Average (4)
  "More lecture would help. More explanation of how to do the problems, not just examples. When exams come, I can usually do the problems assigned or worked in class but the new ones are completely foreign."

- Far Below Average (2)
  "Inability of the instructor to communicate with me during the lecture.
  He jumps from one thing to another. He is not consistent and he
  does not finish the job. (To help us understand the whole thing.)
  In conclusion, his teaching technique is not right."

Listing student responses in this way has a number of benefits. To
begin, the more positive feedback will be read first, which is not only easier to take, but it will help determine whether students are generally satisfied or dissatisfied. It may also show that some students who are satisfied
have the same concerns as some who are less satisfied. In the comments
listed, one student who rated the course "Above Average" and one who
rated it "Below Average" both said that the exam problems were more difficult than those in the homework. What should be done about this? Is the
homework supposed to prepare the students to do similar problems on
exams, or are the exam problems significantly more difficult to glean out
the students who really understand the material from those who do not?
The instructor needs to decide which goal is appropriate and whether it is
right for this situation.

Adding a Second Dimension. Although simply classifying the student
comments according to their overall course ratings can give the instructor
a more realistic view of his or her teaching, adding another dimension can
show where changes might be made. A matrix can help with this analysis.
One side of the matrix contains the course rating given by the student, and
the other side of the matrix is based on five components often cited as components of effective teaching (see Table 3.1).

To make categorizing and sorting the written comments a little easier,
these components have been slightly modified in the matrix we are using.
"Subject Matter" has replaced "Analytic/Synthetic Approach" to enable sorting written comments that deal with how the student is understanding the
subject matter and how it is presented and assessed. Comments such as,
"Exams were more complex than homework," have to do with how the subject is being tested. "Would rate it higher if I understood more" also relates
to how the subject is coming across.

"Organization/Clarity" remains the same and relates to how well the
students can follow the lectures and how the instructor's teaching matches
their expectations of organization. Comments such as, "Jumps around from
one topic to the next," indicate that students are finding the organization
structure difficult for them to follow.

"Instructor-Group Interaction" and "Instructor-Individual Student
Interaction" have been collapsed into one category: "Interaction." Comments in this area relate to how the instructor gets along with the students
and what kind of rapport he or she has developed with them. When the
comments indicate that the instructor "makes sure students understand,"
this means that he or she is relating to the students in a meaningful way and

Table 3.1. Components of Effective Teaching

Teaching Component	Definition
Analytic/Synthetic Approach	Relates to scholarship, with emphasis on breadth, analytic ability, and conceptual understanding
Organization/Clarity	Relates to skill at presentation, but is subject related, not student related, and not concerned merely with rhetorical skill
Instructor-Group Interaction	Relates to rapport with the class as a whole, sensitivity to class response, and skill at securing active class participation
Instructor-Individual Student Interaction	Relates to mutual respect and rapport between the instructor and the individual student
Dynamism/Enthusiasm	Relates to the flair and infectious enthusiasm that comes with confidence, excitement for the subject, and pleasure in teaching.

Source: Hildebrand, Wilson, and Dienst (1971, p. 18).

probably recognizes when students are not understanding the material. At such points in the class, effective instructors ask questions to clear up any misunderstanding.

"Dynamism/Enthusiasm" remains the same and relates to the instructor's enthusiasm for the subject and for teaching. Comments such as, "Makes me want to learn the material," reflect the student's recognition of your enthusiasm.

Instructors can also create their own matrix using variables and categories that are most meaningful to them. For example, an instructor may wish to use a question about fair grading as the basis for sorting comments. How do comments from those who believe grading has been fair differ from those who say grading has been unfair? Or he or she may want to sort the comments according to the students' rating of whether assignments are clear or the lectures are well organized. The main thing is to determine how the students are reacting to the teaching based on a characteristic that will help the instructor decide what changes he or she may want to make.

One point to keep in mind is that research on student evaluation data indicates that student learning is correlated with the overall course and instructor ratings (Cohen, 1981; Feldman, 1989). That is, the classes in which the students gave the instructor or course higher ratings tended to be the classes in which the students learned more (measured by scoring higher on the external exam).

Creating the Matrix

Table 3.2 shows the comments from the engineering class placed in the matrix according to the rating the student gave the course and the characteristics of effective teaching.

The matrix shows that the students who rated the course higher indicated that the main problems they encountered concerned the exams. For example, students who rated the course above average said, "Exams more complex than homework," and those who rated the course below average said essentially the same thing: "Exam problems harder than homework." These students also had a positive feeling about the instructor: "Makes me want to learn the material." On the other hand, students who rated the course lower seemed to need more assistance in structuring the content and determining what was and was not important—for example, "Jumps from one thing to another." Thus, increased specificity in analyzing the student comments could aid the instructor in determining what instructional adjustments might benefit which students.

Multiple references to the same positive or negative comment should be noted by placing the number of times it was written by the students—for example, "Exams were too long (3)." This will also show how many of the students are concerned about a particular topic or are pleased with a particular instructional technique.

Table 3.2. Written Comments Analysis Grid

Rating	Subject Matter	Organization/ Clarity	Interaction	Dynamism/ Enthusiasm
Excellent				
Above Average	Exams more complex than homework	Exams too long	*Makes sure students understand*	*Makes me want to learn material*
Average	Would rate higher if I were understanding better			
Below Average	Needs more lecture Exam problems harder than homework	Needs more explanation of how to do problems		
Poor	Inability to communicate material to students	Jumps from one thing to another Inconsistent		

Note: The italicized comments are positive; those not italicized are more negative.

Increasing the Usefulness and Frequency of Student Written Comments

Theall and Franklin (1991) have been studying student ratings for teaching improvement for many years and have found that "about 10 percent of a class responds with narrative comments unless an extreme situation arises, whether good or bad. In the extreme cases, comments match quantitative results in terms of frequency and intensity, but in more 'normal' situations (that is, 'average' ratings in courses with normal distributions of scores) comments usually come from either the very satisfied or the very dissatisfied" (p. 87). It is easy to overinterpret these few comments and blow the negative comments out of proportion and think, "All of my students say I'm a terrible teacher" (when only five of fifty students made such comments).

To increase the usefulness and frequency of student comments, prompts can be used. In some departments, the following three questions are printed (with space between them) in the comments section of the evaluation form:

- What helped your learning the most in this class?
- What hindered your learning the most in this class?
- What suggestions for changes do you have that would have improved your learning in this class?

An instructor could also put these prompts on the board or overhead and ask the students to respond to them if they are not printed on the response sheet itself. Students tend to write more and provide constructive comments when the prompts are provided than when they are not. Or an instructor might use the categories shown in Table 3.2 and encourage the students to comment on whichever of the topic areas they felt had some meaning for them. Many instructors already take this step by appending some specific course-related questions to the standard forms. This practice helps the students structure their written comments more succinctly and yet more completely because it triggers their thinking about what is of interest to the instructor. Of course, it is good to make one category an open-ended item in which any other comments may be made.

The Happy Ending

The combination of these techniques for analyzing and improving student written comments can help instructors gain insights into how different students learn best in a given course so that instructional efforts can be more tailored to their needs. It has the added advantage of keeping instructors from overreacting to a single negative comment, a constant of human behavior in reaction to evaluation. Finally, it can help instructors avoid the frustration of dealing with seemingly contradictory comments, which might be giving student evaluations the undeserved reputation for unreliability. In the end, instructors will find that bringing a little order to the chaos of written responses will reveal the treasure of information they can provide.

References

Cohen, P. A. "Student Ratings of Instruction and Student Achievement: A Meta-Analysis of Multisection Validity Studies." *Review of Educational Research,* 1981, *51,* 281–309.

Feldman, K. A. "The Association Between Student Ratings of Specific Instructional Dimensions and Student Achievement: Refining and Extending the Synthesis of Data from Multisection Validity Studies." *Research in Higher Education,* 1989, *30,* 583–645.

Hildebrand, M., Wilson, R. C., and Dienst, E. R. *Evaluating University Teaching.* Berkeley: Center for Research and Development in Higher Education, University of California, 1971.

Patton, M. Q. *Qualitative Evaluation and Research Methods.* Thousand Oaks, Calif.: Sage, 1990.

Philipsen, G. "The Qualitative Case Study as a Strategy in Communication Inquiry." *Communicator,* 1982, *12,* 4–17.

Theall, M., and Franklin, J. (1991). "Using Student Ratings for Teaching Improvement." In M. Theall and J. Franklin (eds.), *Effective Practices for Improving Teaching.* New Directions for Teaching and Learning, no. 48. San Francisco: Jossey-Bass, 1991.

Wulff, D. H., and Nyquist, J. D. (2001). "Using Qualitative Methods to Generate Data for Instructional Development." In K. G. Lewis and J. P. Lunde (eds.), *Face to Face: A Sourcebook of Individual Consultation Techniques for Faculty/Instructional Developers.* Stillwater, Okla.: New Forums Press, 2001.

KARRON G. LEWIS is associate director and faculty program coordinator of the Center for Teaching Effectiveness at the University of Texas at Austin.

4

It is the third week of class, and things are not going as well as you would like. You are not sure what might be wrong, but the students are looking either lost or bored. How can you find out what is happening now, before the end of the semester, when students usually fill out their evaluation forms?

Using Midsemester Student Feedback and Responding to It

Karron G. Lewis

Anyone who has tried a new teaching technique in the classroom realizes the complexity of educational research. What works for one teacher may not work for another. What worked in the 9:30 class may not work in the 10:30 class. Methods of teaching that stimulated students in the 1980s may miss the mark with students in the 2000s. One of the few ways for instructors to survive all of this complexity is to continuously evaluate what is happening in the classroom.

In their *Practical Handbook for College Teachers,* Fuhrman and Grasha (1983) stress that the evaluation process must have the following characteristics if it is to improve teaching and learning:

• Evaluation must be continuous. You need to know where you have been and how you are progressing. Changing teaching behaviors is often a slow and painstaking task. Thus, you need to check regularly to monitor for improvement and be encouraged by even small signs of progress.

• Evaluation must be broadly based. To discover yourself as a teacher, you need feedback on all aspects of your teaching: methods (lectures, discussion, group work), support methods (handouts, reading lists, syllabus, homework), and assessment techniques (tests, papers, presentations). You also need to use written response forms as well as informal conversations with students, and you need some idea of what happens to your students both in and out of the classroom.

• Evaluation must be descriptive and diagnostic. It is much more beneficial to know specifics (for example, that you mumbled, used too much technical language, or left too little time for questions) than to hear that the class is boring or useless. Thus, the questions you ask and the forms you use for obtaining feedback need to be fairly focused.

• Evaluation must reflect your personal goals. The purpose of this evaluation is for you to find out about your classes, not to compare yourself with your colleagues. How well you are doing depends on your personal goals and objectives. You also need to take into account your personal style, your discipline, and the environment in which you teach in order for you to determine how effective your teaching actually is.

Exhibit 4.1. Classroom Reaction Survey

I would like to know your reactions to today's class. Please read each of the statements below and circle the letter correponding to the response that best matches your reaction in today's class. Your choices are:

    a. No improvement is needed. (Terrific! This works for me. Keep it up!)
    b. Little improvement is needed. (Maybe a ragged edge or two, but don't lose any sleep over it.)
    c. Improvement is needed. (Not awful, but this merits some attention.)
    d. Considerable improvement is needed. (This is causing me problems. Please help.)

Today, the instructor . . .

a b c d   1. Limited what was covered to a manageable amount of material.
a b c d   2. Made it clear why the material might be important.
a b c d   3. Told us what we would be expected to do with the material (memorize it, use it to solve problems, or whatever.)
a b c d   4. Highlighted key ideas or questions.
a b c d   5. Presented plenty of good examples to clarify difficult material.
a b c d   6. Provided enough variety to keep us reasonably alert.
a b c d   7. Found ways to let us know whether we were understanding the material.
a b c d   8. Helped us summarize the main ideas we were supposed to take away from class.
a b c d   9. Let us know how we might be tested on the material.
a b c d 10. Provided exercises or an assignment so that we could practice using the material.

11. What is your overall rating of today's class?

    A. Excellent
    B. Good
    C. Satisfactory
    D. Fair
    E. Poor

12. What made you rate today's class as high as you did?

13. What kept you from rating today's class higher?

Source: Erickson and Strommer (1991, p. 105).

This evaluation process can be strengthened by obtaining frequent feedback, which enables you to gauge more effectively what your students are learning and how well your teaching techniques and strategies are working.

Classroom Surveys

One simple way to acquire feedback on your teaching is through the use of brief surveys or evaluation forms. These forms can be used at any time during the semester and can be tailored to ask the questions for which you are interested in getting feedback. (Exhibits 4.1 and 4.2 provide samples of this type of survey form.) The survey results can be analyzed quickly, and you can usually make immediate adjustments in your teaching that will facilitate the learning of students and address some of their concerns.

Exhibit 4.2. Teacher Evaluation Form

Teacher's name: _____ Date: _____

Directions: Circle Y (yes) if the statement is **always** or **usually** true.
Circle N (no) if the statment is **never** or **seldom** true.
In multiple choice statements, check the appropriate space.

1. This teacher speaks clearly . . . . Y . . . N
2. This teacher explains things clearly . . . . Y . . . N
3. This teacher is stimulating and interesting to listen to. . . . . Y . . . N
4. The material presented is well organized . . . . Y . . . N
5. This teacher assumes the students know more than they actually do . . . . . Y . . . N
6. This teacher's explanations are:
   a. ___ too technical   b. ___ too simplified   c. ___ satisfactory
7. Time spent on lecturing:
   a. ___ too much   b. ___ too little   c. ___ satisfactory
8. This teacher helps me understand the subject matter . . . . Y . . . N
9. This teacher encourages participation . . . . Y . . . N
10. The class (under this teacher) was paced:
    a. ___ too fast   b. ___ too slow   c. ___ satisfactory

Overall Evaluation

1. My learning in this class is **enhanced** by:

2. My learning in this class is **hindered** by:

3. Suggestions for improvement:

Exhibit 4.3. Teaching Analysis by Students, Form B

Instructor: _____ Class: _____
Date: _____

Instructions to Student

In this inventory you are asked to assess your instructor's specific classroom behaviors. Your instructor has requested this information for purposes of instructional analysis and improvement. Please try to be both thoughtful and candid in your responses so as to maximize the value of the feedback.

Please read each statement carefully and decide the extent to which you feel your instructor does not or does need improvement. Please respond to each statement by selecting one of the following:

A—No improvement needed (very good or excellent performance)
B—Little improvement needed (generally good performance)
C—Improvement needed (generally mediocre performance)
D—Considerable improvement needed (generally poor performance)
E—Not a necessary skill for this course.

Please make your decisions about the need for improvement on the basis of what you think would be best for this particular course and your particular learning style. Try to assess each behavior independently rather than letting your overall impression of the instructor determine each individual rating.

THE INSTRUCTOR'S PERFORMANCE IN . . . (Please circle the letter corresponding to your response.)

1. making effective use of class time .... A B C D E
2. making clear the purposes of each class session and learning activity .... A B C D E
3. integrating the various topics treated in the course .... A B C D E
4. making clear the distinction between major and minor topics ...... A B C D E
5. adjusting the rate at which ideas are covered so that I can follow and understand them .... A B C D E
6. clarifying material which needs explanation .... A B C D E
7. wrapping things up before moving on to a new topic .... A B C D E
8. assigning useful readings and homework .... A B C D E
9. maintaining an atmosphere which actively encourages learning .... A B C D E
10. responding to questions raised by students .... A B C D E
11. inspiring excitement or interest in the content of the course .... A B C D E
12. using a variety of teaching techniques .... A B C D E
13. taking appropriate action if students appear to be bored .... A B C D E
14. asking thought-provoking questions .... A B C D E
15. getting students to participate in class discussions or activities ..... A B C D E
16. relating to students in ways which promote mutual respect .... A B C D E
17. explaining what is expected from each student .... A B C D E
18. making clear precisely how my performance will be evaluated ..... A B C D E
19. designing evaluation procedures which are consistent with course goals .... A B C D E
20. keeping me informed about how well I am doing .... A B C D E

(over)

Section II—(Please circle the letter corresponding to your response.)

21. How much do you think you are learning so far in this course?
    (Please tell **why** you responded the way you did in the space to the right of the options.)
    a. A great deal
    b. A fair amount
    c. Very little
    d. Nothing

22. In your judgment, how important is what you are being asked to learn in this course?
    (Please tell **why** you responded the way you did in the space to the right of the options.)
    a. Very important
    b. Somewhat important
    c. Not very important
    d. Not at all important

23. In comparison to other instructors you have had (in high school and college), how do you rate the effectiveness of this instructor?
    (Please tell **why** you responded the way you did in the space to the right of the options.)
    a. One of the most effective (top 10%)
    b. More effective than most (top 30%)
    c. About average (middle 40%)
    d. Not as effective as most (lower 30%)
    e. One of the least effective (lowest 10%)

24. So far, what is your overall rating of this course?
    (Please tell **why** you responded the way you did in the space to the right of the options.)
    a. Excellent
    b. Good
    c. Satisfactory
    d. Fair
    e. Poor

25. What specific thing would help you most to better understand the material of the course?

Source: Adapted from the Teaching Analysis by Students (TABS) of the Clinic to Improve University Teaching, University of Massachusetts at Amherst (1974). Use of TABS B is granted to the University of Nebraska-Lincoln Teaching and Learning Center by Glenn Erickson, director, Instructional Development Program, University of Rhode Island, Kingston, Rhode Island. (Minor modifications of TABS B made by Joyce Povlacs, instructional consultant, UNL Teaching and Learning Center.)

The Teaching Analysis by Students (TABS) form also provides information on what is going well and what could be changed to make learning more effective (see Exhibit 4.3). One of the benefits of this form is that the last four questions request that students indicate why they rated the question the way they did. These responses can provide specific information and possible ways to help the students learn more effectively. By adding up the number of students who indicated that "little or no improvement is needed" and those who indicate "improvement or much improvement is needed," you can create a bar chart or a table of the percentage of students who chose each response to share with the students. Sometimes students are surprised at the results of this analysis. Frequently, a very vocal but negative student may realize that he or she may be the only person who thinks things are not going well. On the other hand, you may find a particular area, such as your communication or interaction style, that may be hindering student learning.[1]

To obtain feedback from your students concerning their learning, consider using classroom assessment techniques (CATs) in student evaluation feedback (Angelo and Cross, 1993), discussed in the article by Lieberman, Bowers, and Moore in this volume. These may be used frequently and can elicit specific feedback about what students are learning (or not learning) and how you are facilitating or hindering that learning. Some faculty members use one-minute papers or what is referred to as the Muddiest Point CATs at the end of each class session.[2] This information enables them to keep on top of student misunderstandings and questions and indicates to students that the instructor is concerned about their learning.

Several other quick yet highly informative feedback methods can also be used frequently. One asks the students to provide one or two things that you should start, stop, and continue. Encourage the students to provide very specific suggestions (see the article by Svinicki in this volume for ideas for specific feedback). Another quick possibility asks students to respond to the following questions:

- What in the class so far has helped your learning the most or do you like the best?
- What in the class so far has hindered your learning?
- What suggestions do you have to alleviate the problems or concerns listed in the second question?

Procedures for Obtaining Midsemester Feedback

Midsemester feedback is a tool to give teachers and students information on how the class is going and what might be done to make it a better learning environment. These techniques provide a way to find out what students are thinking before the end-of-the-semester evaluation. If you use these techniques, you have to be willing to respond to the information you receive. If you ask a question, be sure you can handle a negative as well as a positive response to that question. If not, do not ask it.

Prepare your students. At the beginning of the class period or at the prior class meeting, let them know what you are going to do and why you are asking for information. Their responses need to be as anonymous as possible, and you need to assure them that this is only to help you improve the learning environment. One faculty member I know uses CATs at the end of every class and asks students to sign their names. He then can individualize feedback and use the filled-out forms to take attendance; they count as part of the students' participation grade. This procedure does not seem to have had any ill effects on the feedback or on his final evaluations.

Be sure the students understand the procedure for filling out the survey. Especially with the Class Reaction Survey and the TABS form (see Exhibits 4.1 and 4.3, respectively), go over the response options. They are not the same as most other surveys include; they ask whether improvement is needed rather than rating the item from Excellent to Poor.

After the students have responded, collect their responses, and read through them immediately after class if possible. Analyze the responses by noting how many times the same types of problems crop up and how many students responded to each response option. As you read the responses, consider how you might make changes, if indicated, and why you might not make some of the changes students request. Jot down your thoughts as you analyze the materials to help you compose the response you will share with the students.

Responding to the Students

Perhaps the most important part of conducting a midsemester feedback session is your response to the students. In your response, you need to let them know what you learned from their information and what differences it will make. For some of the items you will be able to report, "Forty-five percent of you thought that X was something that was really impeding your learning and that I need to change. I've considered what I might do differently, and here's what I've decided." Also be sure to point out the positive comments and the number of students who made them. Let the students know what adjustments, if any, you are making in your teaching as a result of the information they provided, and tell the students of adjustments they might make in their behavior to improve their learning. If you have done midsemester evaluations in previous years, talk to the students about how you have used these past comments and ratings to make changes in your classes. This openness will encourage them to be honest and more specific in their responses.

Case Study. To better understand how this process works, let's consider a concrete example of using midsemester evaluations. Here is a description of what happened to one instructor as a result of taking the time to gather data from the students while the class was still intact.

Dr. Brown was teaching a math class during the spring semester, and the end-of-semester evaluations from the students were quite low (2.3 to 3.0 on a 5.0-point scale). At the middle of the following fall semester, he decided to conduct a midsemester feedback session to see if this year's students felt the same way as last year's. He chose to use the TABS form so he could find out what students thought he was doing well and what he was not doing so well. Figure 4.1 shows the results for the responses to the evaluation in the fall class and in the spring class, after he had made changes in his teaching and conducted the same evaluation. The items that the students rated are given in Table 4.1.

The ratings for the fall semester indicate that the students were quite satisfied with Dr. Brown's teaching on most of the items. However, over half of the students felt that changes needed to be made in the areas assessed by items 11, 12, 13, 14, and 15. These five items deal with using a variety of teaching techniques and the ability to get students interested in the material. Dr. Brown discussed these results with a faculty development consultant, and together they came up with some changes in his teaching that might address the students' concerns. He also looked on the Web for resources that related to enthusiasm, various teaching techniques, and getting students involved in the class.

He decided to try using more active learning techniques (such as think-pair-share and group activities) that could be accomplished easily and without consuming much time. (In the think-pair-share procedure, students are given a problem or question to consider. They first *think* about it themselves and try to come up with a solution or answer. Then they discuss their solution in a *pair* with another student sitting nearby. After they have compared solutions and reached a level of agreement on the final solution, they are invited to *share* their solution with the whole class during an open discussion.) He decided to try asking the students to write one-minute papers at the end of class periodically to help him judge whether they were understanding the material and whether they had any questions.

He discussed the student responses and his ideas for change with his class about one week after they had filled out the feedback forms. He thus had time to think about what to focus on in his discussion and make transparencies of the graphs of the results to share. During this class session, he also asked for student comments and reactions. His openness encouraged students to participate and indicated to them that he was serious about responding to the information they had provided.

At the end of the fall semester Dr. Brown's end-of-semester evaluations were quite a bit better than they were the previous spring. During the midsemester break, he worked on incorporating more active learning strategies into his plans for the class, and around the middle of the following spring semester he again administered the TABS form to his students. The spring data in Figure 4.1 show that the percentage of students who said he did not need improvement on items 11 through 14 increased, and those who said he did need improvement on those items decreased. The only item that is a little puzzling is item 15 ("Getting students to participate in class discussion or activities"), which changed rather dramatically. He and the consultant surmised that this change occurred because he was trying to incorporate more active learning techniques, and now the students wanted to be involved even more. The overall ratings of the instructor and course

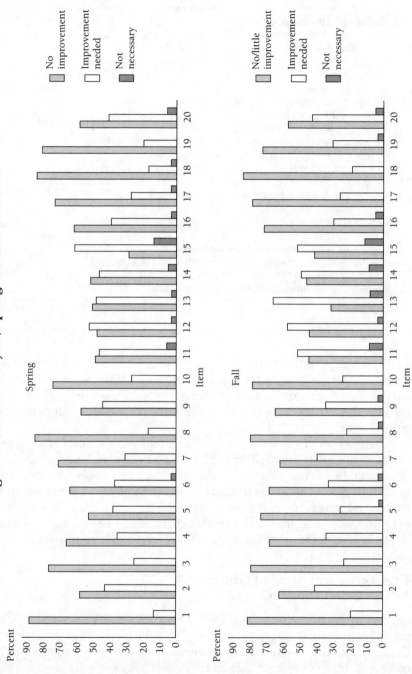

Figure 4.1. TABS Analysis, Spring and Fall Semesters

Table 4.1. TABS Items

1. Making effective use of class time
2. Making clear the purposes of each class session and learning activity
3. Integrating the various topics treated in the course
4. Making clear the distinction between major and minor topics
5. Adjusting the rate at which ideas are covered so that I can follow and understand them
6. Clarifying material which needs explanation
7. Wrapping things up before moving on to a new topic
8. Assigning useful readings and homework
9. Maintaining an atmosphere which actively encourages learning
10. Responding to questions raised by students
11. Inspiring excitement or interest in the content of the course
12. Using a variety of teaching techniques
13. Taking appropriate action if students appear to be bored
14. Asking thought-provoking questions
15. Getting students to participate in class discussions or activities
16. Relating to students in ways which promote mutual respect
17. Explaining what is expected from each student
18. Making clear precisely how my performance will be evaluated
19. Designing evaluation procedures which are consistent with course goals
20. Keeping me informed about how well I am doing

showed some improvement too (see Table 4.2): a small shift toward more positive ratings.

The written comments on items 23 and 24 indicate that the primary way Dr. Brown could help the students understand the content more effectively would be to provide more examples and work more problems in class. Because this math course is primarily a skills course, the comment is not surprising.

Discussion of the Case Study. Thus, midsemester feedback can provide a great deal of information concerning how the students feel the class is going and how much they think they are learning. By using the data gathered from this form, an instructor can discover where changes might be made to address some of the concerns of the students. Each class is different, though, so you need to remember that and not be discouraged when large changes in the students' responses are not immediately evident.

Oral Feedback: Student Group Instructional Diagnosis

Feedback does not have to be written. Using the process known as student group instructional diagnosis, a peer or someone from your instructional development center can elicit verbal feedback from your students. In this technique, the peer or instructional consultant comes to your class and asks students to form small groups of four or five to discuss the following three questions:

Table 4.2. Spring Ratings of Instructor and Course

	Fall Rating	Spring Rating
Item 23: "In comparison to other instructors you have had, how do you rate the effectiveness of this instructor?"		
a. One of the most effective	11%	11%
b. More effective than most	25	29
c. About average	48	35
d. Not as effective as most	13	20
e. One of the least effective	3	5
Item 24: "So far, what is your overall rating of this course?"		
a. Excellent	14	20
b. Good	34	31
c. Satisfactory	34	27
d. Fair	15	13
e. Poor	3	9

- What in the class so far has helped your learning the most or do you like the best?
- What in the class so far has hindered your learning?
- What suggestions do you have to alleviate the problems or concerns listed in the second question?

Each group is given a sheet of paper on which to record their responses to the questions. After about ten minutes, the students reconvene as a large group, and one member of each small group reports what the group consensus was for each of the three questions. These are written on an overhead transparency by the consultant or peer. When there seems to be disagreement, the consultant asks for a show of hands to determine the approximate percentage of students who feel one way or the other. The student feedback is then summarized by the consultant or peer and shared with the instructor. This process keeps the feedback anonymous, since the consultant or peer does not know the students. After the comments have been shared, the instructor thanks the students for their participation and discusses what changes will be made.

Conclusion

You do not have to wait until the middle of a semester to ask for feedback. Getting feedback as soon as the third or fourth week can be useful as well as informative and provides plenty of time to make any changes. By engaging in this process early, you build rapport with the students. They see that you are interested in their ideas and suggestions and that you will take them into consideration. After you have had some time to make a few changes, gather more information, using the same form again, to see whether the learning environment has improved.

Remember the four characteristics of the evaluation process discussed at the beginning of this article:

• Evaluation must be continuous.
• Evaluation must be broadly based.
• Evaluation must be descriptive and diagnostic.
• Evaluation must reflect your personal goals.

By keeping these characteristics in mind, you will be able to design feedback mechanisms that will help you constantly improve your teaching.

Notes

1. Additional midsemester feedback forms may be found on the Web site of the Center for Teaching Effectiveness at the University of Texas at Austin: www.utexas.edu /academic/cte/getfeedback.

2. To use a one-minute paper, the instructor stops class two or three minutes early and asks students to respond briefly to some variation on the following two questions: "What was the most important thing you learned during this class?" and "What important question remains unanswered?" Students write their responses on index cards or half-sheets of paper and hand them in. The instructor quickly goes over the responses, summarizes the number of "most important things" and analyzes the questions, and then takes two or three minutes at the beginning of the next class session to address these responses.

The Muddiest Point is probably the simplest CAT to use. It provides high information return for low investment of time and energy. At the end of class (or at the end of a topic or unit), ask the students to jot down a quick response to the question, "What was the muddiest point in [a lecture, a discussion, a homework assignment, a play, or a film]?" The instructor reviews the answers and explains the one or two muddiest points further.

References

Angelo, T. A., and Cross, K. P. *Classroom Assessment Techniques: A Handbook for College Teachers.* (2nd ed.) San Francisco: Jossey-Bass, 1993.

Erickson, B. L., and Strommer, D. W. *Teaching College Freshmen.* San Francisco: Jossey-Bass, 1991.

Fuhrman, B. S., and Grasha, A. F. *A Practical Handbook for College Teachers.* New York: Little, Brown, 1983.

KARRON G. LEWIS is associate director and faculty program coordinator of the Center for Teaching Effectiveness at the University of Texas at Austin.

5

Feedback from classroom assessment techniques can provide informative and useful information about teaching and student learning. Adapting these techniques for technology provides even more opportunity for students to provide input.

Use of Electronic Tools to Enhance Student Evaluation Feedback

Devorah Lieberman, Nancy Bowers, David R. Moore

Classroom assessment techniques (CATs; Angelo and Cross, 1993), an important form of student feedback, continue to gain acceptance as effective methods for improving instruction. These techniques are meant to inform instructors about which teaching strategies are effective, and they can be used to provide immediate feedback to students on their own learning. Instructors are encouraged to use these data for midcourse modification with the intention of improving their teaching strategies to meet student learning needs. The ultimate goal is to achieve desired student learning outcomes and meet course objectives more effectively.

One way to conceptualize how CATs fit into the overall evaluation and assessment of teaching and learning is outlined in Figure 5.1. Most courses typically consist of a set of course objectives, which guide the overall course design and course activities (Pregent, 1994). Student learning objectives are those outcomes (for example, content, knowledge process skills, or attitudes) that are identified by the instructor and should be achieved by each student by the end of the course. The teaching strategies are those media or modes that the instructor selects to convey the information that students are expected to learn. These areas are very much interrelated, and consideration of these relationships is crucial for teaching excellence.

There are three possible approaches to the evaluation and assessment of teaching effectiveness and student learning. Two of these are traditional elements of evaluation that occur within any course. One is instructor evaluation of student learning, which is usually accomplished through exams, term papers, projects, and portfolios. The instructor may use this information for purposes of student grading or ranking. The second traditional

Figure 5.1. The Relationship Among Course Design Components and Evaluative and Assessment Components

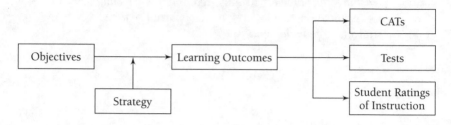

approach is students' evaluation of their instructor's teaching. Such data are usually externally driven and are kept in the instructor's files (and in the institution's files on the instructor, to be used for administrative purposes and personnel decisions).

CATs are an approach that not all instructors may be aware of, yet this student feedback has tremendous potential for assessing and improving teaching and resultant student outcomes. For example, instructors frequently assume that the modes of information delivery they have selected are those most likely to guide the students to the identified student learning outcomes. Rarely do instructors ask themselves why they chose a particular mode of teaching or why they assume this strategy is the best route to achieving a particular student learning outcome. CATs allow instructors to gather this information quickly and use it to guide midcourse corrections or modifications in their teaching strategies. Design, delivery, and analysis of CATs can be greatly enhanced through the use of electronic tools, and pairing of CATs with the appropriate technology can also lead to results that may be more valid than traditional paper-and-pencil teacher evaluation forms completed at the end of the term.

Basic Classroom Assessment Techniques

There are hundreds of well developed CATs available for instructors to choose from (Angelo and Cross, 1993). Those discussed here serve only as representative examples.

An assignment matrix or a teaching strategy matrix are two mechanisms by which instructors can receive formative student feedback on their teaching (Lieberman, 1999). The assignment matrix (Exhibit 5.1) allows students to comment (on a scale of 1 to 5) on the degree to which they perceive the success of particular class assignments in relation to the expected student learning outcomes. An added benefit in this process is that the initial construction of the matrix serves to remind the instructor of the original intentions in matching a particular assignment with specific student learning outcomes. The teaching strategy matrix (Exhibit 5.2) follows a

Exhibit 5.1. Assignment Matrix

Student Learning Objectives	Course Assignment 1	Course Assignment 2	Course Assignment 3	Course Assignment 4	Course Assignment 5
Objective 1					
Objective 2					
Objective 3					

Exhibit 5.2. Teaching Strategy Matrix

Student Learning Objectives	Teaching Strategy 1 (lecture)	Teaching Strategy 2 (group work)	Teaching Strategy 3 (Internet search)	Teaching Strategy 4 (class discussion)	Teaching Strategy 5 (think-pair-share)
Objective 1					
Objective 2					
Objective 3					

similar format. Students complete their perceptions of how a particular teaching strategy helped them achieve the related learning outcomes. Instructors can use the results from CATs such as these to ascertain if students perceive that assignments were related to course learning and which teaching strategies are perceived as the most related to student learning objectives.

A number of short CATs (see Angelo and Cross, 1993) are designed to be delivered during the last few minutes of class or at the beginning of class. They are typically anonymous and are frequently used to assess a specific class session. For example, after completing a lecture just prior to the end of class, an instructor may ask the students to write down the muddiest point of the lecture. Or the students may be asked to summarize in their own words an important concept covered during the lecture. These types of CATs may be informative not only to the instructor but to the students as well. Compilation of the results can be distributed to the students, and they can compare their own learning and comprehension with that of the rest of the class. Analysis of CATs may be taken one step further: instructors can share with their students any modifications they decide to make in their teaching as a direct outcome of the results of the CATs.

Electronic Implementation of CATs

CATs are typically completed during class using a pencil-and-paper approach. The use of an electronic tool to facilitate the implementation of a CAT, referred to as a technoCAT (Lieberman, 1998), allows an instructor to rapidly collect and analyze formative student feedback concerning teaching and learning. Furthermore, technoCATs can easily be completed asynchronously by allowing the students to post their responses on a course Web site. For example, each student could complete the strategy and assignment matrixes on-line and electronically submit them to the instructor. With appropriate software, results can be recorded immediately, and data for each student learning objective by course assignment or the data for each student learning objective by teaching strategy can be summarized.

TechnoCATs have the potential to provide instructors with more options and freedom to collect data about student learning in relation to their student learning objectives. The assessment process may take place in class or out of class depending on the intent of the instructor and the available technology. We recognize two potentially important advantages of using technoCATs. First, because of the way they use technology, they may allow for more data collection using less in-class time. Second, they can allow for time for students to reflect on their responses in the convenience of their own home (or residence hall room) or in a computer lab. TechnoCATs are powerful tools to gather the information about student learning in relation to specific teaching strategies at any time during the term.

Electronic Tools for Asynchronous Classroom Assessment. Asynchronous assessment tools are those that do not require both the student and professor to be present in the same space at the same time. These tools may be best suited for courses that are conducted using the Internet or other forms of distributed education. The asynchronous evaluation medium may also be appropriate for shifting assessment outside the classroom to preserve class time for contact between students and instructor. Tools such as e-mail, discussion bulletin boards, and on-line quizzes and surveys can all be used in an asynchronous mode to gather feedback.

Electronic Tools for Synchronous Classroom Assessment. Paper-and-pencil CATs are typically conducted at a single site with the professor in the room. These synchronous technoCATs may be conducted when the students are located at the same site as the professor or they are communicating in real time from a distance. The technology is used in a way that permits all the students to complete the assessment and return it digitally at the same time, regardless of whether they are all physically at the same location. One advantage of a synchronous technoCAT would be that if a student had a question or if the assessment had open-ended questions, simultaneous communication with the individual administering the technoCAT would still be possible.

Hand-held feedback devices are an example of a set of powerful electronic tools for conducting synchronous technoCATs. Networked and wireless hand-held devices may be a mechanism for students to provide immediate feedback to the instructor concerning their learning or their perceptions of instructor effectiveness. A successful tool for offering such feedback is the Perception Analyzer (www.cinfo.com), created and marketed by Columbia Information Systems. The Perception Analyzer comprises individual hand-held devices that students use to deliver immediate feedback during class. Students can view questions simultaneously as their responses are projected on the screen. A summary of the feedback can be saved and printed out later or viewed immediately on a monitor while the instructor is teaching. The instructor can use this feedback immediately to modify current or future presentations. Synchronous electronic tools such as the Perception Analyzer can provide dynamic, continuous, formative feedback.

Scenarios Using TechnoCATs

Selecting the appropriate tool to conduct a particular technoCAT depends on a number of factors and variables. Different instructional circumstances and different technoCATs require technologies with a variety of attributes. One technology may have advantages in one context and be cumbersome in another. We present a series of scenarios concerning the use of technoCATs in an attempt to assist instructors in selecting the appropriate approach.

Uncomfortable with Complex Technology or Little Extra Class Time. A business leadership professor has decided to use the Muddiest Point CAT (Angelo and Cross, 1993), a technique that consists of asking students to respond to the question, "What was the muddiest point from today's lecture?" Her class always seems to run long, and her students are usually packed up and ready to go before she has finished. She has used this technique in discussion courses and thinks the feedback would be valuable. Her students have Internet access, but many do not have up-to-date computers. This instructor has limited experience with technology herself. Which technology should she use to conduct this CAT?

On the basis of her constraints—no time in class; a need for easy-to-use, ubiquitous technology; and the open-ended nature of her chosen CAT—it makes most sense for her to consider using e-mail for the technoCAT. Using this tool, she assigns the Muddiest Point to the students as a homework assignment. Her students then have an opportunity to respond after they have reviewed their notes and digested the material. Once this instructor receives the students' e-mail, she adjusts her lecture accordingly or sends a blanket response based on the most commonly occurring or most troublesome questions.

Experienced with Technology and Teaching at a Distance. An art professor wants to know whether his students are able to distinguish art nouveau from art deco. To this end, he has chosen the Defining Features Matrix CAT, which requires students to categorize concepts according to the presence or absence of important defining features (Angelo and Cross, 1993). The class is primarily a Web-based course and makes heavy use of discussion forums. This instructor has a great deal of experience using technology to teach and chooses an electronic survey, which is part of the Web course package he is already using to teach. He creates a matching question that is automatically collated and saves him the time of hand grading all the responses.

Sharing the Results Immediately with Students in Class. A sociology professor is interested in her students' ability to identify major technological developments and the resultant impacts on social systems. Specifically, she is interested in her students' perception of the relationship between these factors. She teaches in a technology-friendly classroom and is quite comfortable with computer-based technologies, and has therefore decided to use a concept mapping software package. She uses the software to create a graphical representation of how facts, concepts, and social rules relate to one another during the class session. Students can immediately tell the instructor how they see the various components relating to one another. This technoCAT allows the instructor and the students concurrently to view these relationships as they develop and evolve. Misconceptions can be identified and corrected using this technique. Equally important is the opportunity to review and study these relationships after the fact, since the data are collected and stored electronically.

Using Commercial Courseware to Conduct or Augment a Course. Consider a variety of techniques for incorporating technoCATs into a course. Many commercially available software packages facilitate the design and delivery of Web-based instructional materials. The password-protected environment within these course environments facilitates both synchronous and asynchronous application of technoCATs without the risk of participation by individuals not enrolled in the course. Usually, there are a number of computer-mediated communication tools within these environments that can be used to deliver technoCATs:

• A prior knowledge probe using an on-line quiz tool. A biology instructor is using a commercial courseware package to supplement an upper-division course in molecular biology. Each year, the instructor has a large number of students who are not adequately prepared, despite prerequisites for the course. In an effort to identify these students, the instructor creates a prior knowledge probe using the system's quiz tool. The students are required to complete this questionnaire on-line during the first week of the course. The prior knowledge probe is not graded, but is designed to provide rich feedback for the students, as well as important information for the instructor. The system grades the questionnaire immediately, and the students receive feedback (such as remedial assignments or suggestions on where to get more information) for each question they answered incorrectly. Students who do particularly poorly may be advised to drop the course and instead take a course that will provide a fuller foundation. The instructor receives a summary of the results delineating his students' strengths and weaknesses, allowing him to adjust the amount of time he spends covering certain material.

• Anonymous student feedback using the course bulletin board. An instructor in sociology uses a commercial courseware package to support a face-to-face course. In previous courses, she found the use of weekly CATs to be valuable, but the time taken away from lecture was too great. She discovers that the bulletin board provided by the commercial courseware can be configured to allow anonymous postings, and she creates a forum specifically for her weekly technoCATs. She finds that her students are more likely to participate honestly and thoughtfully when they complete the techno-CATs anonymously and without the time pressure of completing them in class. Students use the bulletin board tool to share their feelings about their learning and their attitudes toward her instruction. Furthermore, she can use the bulletin board tool to post a summary of the issues raised by each week's technoCAT and any actions she chooses to take as a result. This type of technoCAT allows her to examine student learning and her own teaching strategies, and it empowers her students by letting them become involved in their own education.

• Synchronous student feedback using a chatroom. A geography instructor who is using commercial courseware to deliver an entirely on-line course is concerned about developing a sense of community among his students. He would like to conduct his technoCATs in a manner that would draw his students closer together. His class is small so he decides to conduct his CATs in real time using the courseware's chatroom tool, especially since he can configure the chatroom to let his students participate anonymously. This arrangement allows him to come "together" with his students on a weekly basis to complete a variety of technoCATs in a synchronous manner, similar to that in traditional face-to-face courses. Students share their views with each other and with him, and he is immediately able to address any concerns and issues that are raised. The technoCAT discussions conducted in this manner may be recorded, which has two benefits: he can share the results with students who were unable to participate, and he can reflect on the results and use them to modify his teaching strategies and, he hopes, improve his on-line learning community.

• Assess student attitudes using an on-line survey. A first-time user of commercial courseware is concerned that her math students are not using all of the material she has provided or that they may be having problems accessing certain portions of her on-line course. She wants to be sure that all students have equal access to the course materials and that the technology she is using is not a barrier to their learning. About three weeks into the term, she realizes that if she assesses her students now, she may be able to modify her use of the courseware environment if necessary. She creates a survey, which students can submit anonymously, to assess their attitudes toward the use of the courseware environment.

When all students have completed the survey on-line, the results are summarized immediately, and she discovers that most of the students are satisfied with her use of the courseware environment. In fact, they indicated that they appreciated the on-line materials she had compiled and that her use of the courseware greatly enhanced their learning experience. Their only suggestion was that they thought it would be useful if she would offer virtual office hours using the course chatroom. The instructor was greatly relieved after reviewing the results and quickly instituted virtual office hours. She found the students to be much more open with her after completing the survey, which she attributed to the fact that they appreciated her willingness to solicit and value their opinions concerning her teaching strategies.

Comfortable with Technology and Teaching a Large Introductory Course. A first-year instructor in chemistry realizes that much of the information she presents in lecture is complex and difficult to grasp. Unfortunately, she has over 150 students, and it is almost impossible for her to determine how much or how little of the material her students are understanding. She knows that if she could continuously evaluate her students' comprehension of the lecture material, she could stop and clarify issues when the class is having problems or move on to a new topic when they are comfortable with their knowledge. She has decided to try hand-held feedback devices to collect continuous, real-time data during her lectures.

Each of her students is given a hand-held device and instructed to provide her feedback on a 5-point scale concerning their level of understanding of the material she presents. The first time she used this feedback system, she was astounded. At strategic points in the lecture, she had the students indicate how much they thought they understood the previous point that was discussed. During the lecture, she was able to view a real-time summary of her students' responses. She found that the students were not understanding parts of her lecture that she thought were perfectly clear. By immediately modifying her approach to the topic, she greatly increased their level of understanding.

CAT or TechnoCAT: How Best to Decide

One important aspect of the use of technoCATs is the choice of medium for delivering CATs in a manner that is flexible, easy, and efficient. It would be easy to fall into the trap of promoting the use of electronic evaluation of technoCATs because of their novelty; they seem trendy. In addition, because the tools may seem cutting edge to students, they may be more inclined to rate the instructor positively (or not).

We propose that the use of technology to either enhance or replace traditional paper-and-pencil evaluation tools follow the principle that new is not always better, but that electronic assessment and evaluation methods should be considered where they are either more efficient or perhaps more reliable than the traditional paper-and-pencil approach. One question that could guide decision making around spending the time, effort, and university resources needed to design and implement electronic assessment and evaluation is, "Is this the best method for addressing that which I intend to assess or evaluate?"

CATs are an invaluable tool for improving teaching and learning. Moreover, the use of electronic tools for delivering and analyzing CATs can be applied across an instructional spectrum, ranging from traditional classroom settings to entirely distance-based courses. Following is a short assessment to help you weigh the pros and cons of technoCATs based on your own needs and constraints:

- Are you constrained for time such that you cannot conduct an in-class CAT?
- In general, are you comfortable with technology?
- Are you familiar with technical tools that may be used for implementing technoCATs?
- Do your students have access to this technology outside the class?
- Are your students comfortable with the technology you plan to use?
- Do you need to provide flexibility in the way students respond to your CAT?
- Is it important that responses to your CAT be anonymous?
- Does the technology you plan to use for your CAT really help you assess what you want to know?
- Do you want to be able to archive or reuse the data you collect from your CAT?
- Do you want to provide your students with immediate feedback based on the CAT results?

If you answered the majority of those questions yes, then the time and effort to implement a technoCAT in one of your courses would probably be quite valuable. If you answer the majority of the questions no, then you may not be ready to incorporate technoCATs into your teaching.[1]

Conclusion

The application of electronic tools to the design and delivery of classroom assessments can greatly strengthen their utility. Selecting the appropriate tool requires careful consideration of the attributes of particular technologies and a clear understanding of course goals and objectives. Many tools may be helpful in one circumstance and counterproductive in another. The more thoughtful and open you are about the design of the technoCATs and the collection of student evaluation feedback, the greater the strides you will make in advancing your teaching and your students' learning.

Note

1. We invite you to participate in our own technoCAT by completing an on-line version of the questionnaire at www.oaa.pdx.edu/CAE/technocat/ or www.oaa.pdx.edu/CAE /technocat/. Readers' summary results will be posted on the Web site. If you are interested, provide your name and e-mail address, and we will share with you a summary of our results.

References

Angelo, T., and Cross, P. *Classroom Assessment Techniques: A Handbook for College Teachers.* (2nd ed.) San Francisco: Jossey-Bass Publishers, 1993.
Columbia Information Systems. "Perception Analyzer." [www.cinfo.com]. 2001.
Lieberman, D. "Using Technology Wisely." *NEA Advocate,* Oct. 1998. [www.nea.org/HE /head/advo/9810/thriving.html]
Lieberman, D. "Evaluating teaching through electronic classroom assessment." In P. Seldin (ed.), *Changing Practices in Evaluating Teaching: A Practical Guide to Improved Faculty Performance and Promotion/Tenure Decisions.* Bolton, Mass.: Anker Publishing Co., 1999.
Pregent, R. *Charting Your Course: How to Prepare to Teach More Effectively.* Madison, Wis.: Magna Publications, 1994.

DEVORAH LIEBERMAN is vice provost and assistant to the president of Campus Initiatives and director of teaching and learning in the Center for Academic Excellence at Portland State University, Oregon.

NANCY BOWERS is an instructional support specialist in instruction and research services at Portland State University, Oregon.

DAVID R. MOORE is the manager of distributed education at Portland State University, Oregon.

6

*Student evaluations can benefit the teacher and students
alike when both strive to make the process more reflective
and collaborative. Student quality teams can serve as a
mediator between the instructor and the students, as well
as a stimulator of better student feedback.*

Taking Student Criticism Seriously: Using Student Quality Teams to Guide Critical Reflection

Larry Spence, Lisa Firing Lenze

"You can't please everyone, so you gotta please yourself." The lyrics of Ricky Nelson's bitter song ran through the mind of Professor David Parkersburg as he walked back to his office after a training session on Continuous Quality Improvement.

The session had set the song thumping, and he realized it had played in his heart for many years. Like most other beginning teachers, Parkersburg had listened to every complaint and criticism that students offered. If assignments were not clear, grading was confusing, or the pace was too fast, he adjusted his techniques. But after the first five years as a professor, he learned that his changes made no difference: students continued to complain. He quit listening to student comments and learned to please himself.

After the session on quality team processes, Parkersburg understood what had happened. His changes did not result in gains in the quality of learning because he had fallen into a quality improvement trap. He had not educated or engaged the students as knowledgeable customers in improving the process of their own learning; he had merely asked their opinions and reacted accordingly. Although students are not qualified to answer some questions about instruction (for example, whether the instructor is an expert in the subject matter), they are qualified to report on how assignments help or inhibit their learning performance. But this is not something they come by naturally; he needed to encourage students' thoughtful and informed review of the things that mattered in his course, and a quality team might be just the mechanism to accomplish that.

Searching the university Web site, Parkersburg found a teaching support unit that promoted course and curriculum innovations aimed at shifting the emphasis of undergraduate education for teaching to learning. When he clicked to the site, he found a heading "Student Quality Teams." He clicked again and found the model for which he was looking. It read, "A Student Quality Team is a group of students in a class that monitors the work processes of the students and the instructor to find opportunities for changes that lead to better learning. 'Monitoring' includes regularly developing, distributing and compiling surveys, and tracking changes throughout the semester. 'Work processes' include any student-instructor interactions, such as lectures, in-class group activities, assignments, or office hours interactions."

Quality circles originated in Japan as a way to get teams of workers and managers directly involved in industrial planning and problem solving. It was also intended to help workers and managers be more reflective about their work so they would be able to make recommendations for process improvement. The idea was adopted by many organizations in the United States in the early 1980s, with sometimes spectacular results. Some faculty members adapted the idea for classroom use, but with mixed results. The most successful model is based on the classroom assessment quality circles described by Angelo and Cross (1993).

Like their industrial counterparts, quality circles or teams in the classroom comprise those most directly involved in the processes of teaching and learning: the instructor and the students. Student quality teams consist of five or six students enrolled in a course, who receive extra credit under the tutelage of a team facilitator (not necessarily part of the course) who meets with them once a week. Instructors charge the team with surveying students enrolled in the course about their learning experiences. Teams may do this using focus groups, one-minute papers, written surveys, and other such data collection methods. Teams or selected members of the team meet periodically with the faculty member to gather and present information and discuss quality improvement ideas. They present their findings to the students either on-line or in class. With adequate training and coaching, a student quality team can collect information on aspects of the teaching-learning process ranging from instructional mechanics to student reflections on their learning. Through this repeated practice over the semester, students enrolled in the course become more adept at expressing critical observations about their learning. This development as critically reflective learners can be an important outgrowth of the quality team process.

Learning to Reflect Critically on Teaching and Learning

Progression toward critical reflection must be both coached and practiced. Students today often experience learning by doing in real life as opposed to the "teach-and-tell" learning required in the classroom.

They seem to be particularly adept at mastering new technological skills with an ease and confidence that startles their elders. And when asked how they learned those skills, they say that they just "sit down and play with it." That expresses the common and successful experience of learning by starting with a task and discovering what you need to know to complete it.

The same can happen with learning to reflect about learning: they need to do it, but they rarely get the chance in a teach-and-tell environment. John Dewey pointed out that the secret of democracy was that it challenged people to decide and thereby educated men and women to think beyond the narrow demands of their own lives. But he added that citizens could not become good at making public decisions unless they actually learned from mistakes and became adept as a result. Thus, the more that citizens are reduced to an audience in a democracy, the less effective this form of government will become.

Similarly, students cannot become good at criticism unless they have opportunities to criticize and live with the consequences. Students need to learn to become good consumers—indeed, to become good learners. Perceiving the learning process as something more than a transmission of information is the first and necessary step. Instituting a regular feedback process such as the quality team approach provides the frequent opportunities that students need to practice and hone their reflective skills.

Stages of Development in Critical Reflection

A lot of mature students still hold on to the old model of learning that says, "You go to school, a smart person tells you something, and you are expected to learn it and remember it. If you do not, you are stupid." That tell-and-test model persists in the minds of many because it is built into the design of classrooms, textbooks, and even the latest cutting-edge Web-based instruction. In that model, the causes for failure are either the teacher, who is at fault, or the student, who is not smart enough to learn what was told. Only as students begin to abandon and modify that model with a more complex representation of learning can they begin to entertain other possible reasons for failure and thereby become better at critical reflection.

In learning to critique a course, students proceed through roughly four stages of leaving that model and creating its replacement: whining, correcting the instructor, learning meaningfully, and reflecting on the way they learn. Each stage represents a strategy for improving the learning situation that does not necessarily coincide with the goals of the instructor. But if instructors guide the process while respecting the autonomy of the students, progress is likely.

If you ask a class of students to critique a course, the first yield will be numerous ways that work can be reduced. They will also demand faculty enthusiasm, humor, and a high degree of fairness and concern. If you resist the temptation to dumb down the course and persist in organizing students to become critics, you can expect some startling improvements.

For example, the second yield will be dozens of suggestions for ways in which the instructor can improve. The suggestions will run to better organization, more examples, a better textbook, less ambiguous questions on tests, and proper pacing of course delivery. Provided you get through with your ego intact and your curiosity whetted, you might move on.

The third yield will be ideas about how to improve the learning tools of the course: examples, explanations, outlines, feedback, and so on. If you use those ideas to focus students on moving from rote memorization to connecting what they learn to their models of reality, then a final yield is likely.

The fourth yield results in more reflective ideas on how students can better use class time, ask better questions, use mind tools like concept maps and diagrams, and proffer ideas on improving assignments to enhance learning.

Using Quality Teams to Respond to Stages of Student Criticism

One way to help students at various stages of critical development is to think more systematically about how to listen and respond in such a way as to move their development to the next higher level.

Stage 1: Complaints. Students report that there's too much work, the text is too difficult, the work is beyond their competence, they need explicit guidelines (what will be on the test?), and so on. The strategy of these complaints is both to reduce the effort required and deflect the threat to students' self-images as smart learners.

Listening Focus. Reflect students' expressions of difficulty: learning is frustrating and painful. Be careful to discuss the complaints and reply (by e-mail, for example) with interpretations concerning the sources of frustration. Do not convey irritation with or lack of concern for what the students are saying. Try to help sort out learning issues from the sounds of pain. It is hard not to be condescending or impatient, so try to remember that last frustrating experience you had programming your VCR.

Actions. Do not change anything. Do respond with discussions (either via e-mail with the individual or with the entire class when students raise a particularly good issue) that focus on learning. When students complain, respond with questions. Are you working smart? How do you schedule your time? How do you read the assignments? Have you read the syllabus? What are the objectives of the course? Why is learning hard, painful, and humiliating at times? What are the payoffs of this course?

Quality Team Actions. Introduce one-minute papers and compile answers for the instructor.

Stage 2: Mechanics. Students report that it's hard to see writing on the board, overheads are difficult to read, lectures are paced too fast or too slow, the materials are boring, the assignments are unclear, grading is confusing, and there is a need for more examples, review sessions, sample exam questions, and so on. The strategy of these comments is to improve the effectiveness of student efforts by getting the instructor to be more helpful.

Listening Focus. See issues to which you can respond by making relatively minor changes in course mechanics and demonstrate that students can make a difference in the course.

Actions. Respond quickly to students' ideas and complaints. Use thicker chalk for writing on the board, increased font sizes for overheads, care with power point designs, and so on. Be sure to announce that you are responding and changing. Have students devise rubrics for grading assignments, arrange library consultations to assist with papers, offer choices of assignments or grading systems, and so on. The changes may seem minor but they represent payoffs for students' proactivity. The message is, "You can make a difference in the way this course is conducted. Walk the talk."

Quality Team Actions. Begin creating surveys and presenting results to the class for discussion.

Stage 3: Process. Students suggest learning helpers such as better examples, outlines, tools, explanations, and faster feedback. The strategy of these responses is to improve the learning in the course, with students moving from memorizing to understanding.

Listening Focus. Look for detailed criticism of specific assignments. How did this reading help or hinder your understanding? How could this paper assignment work better? What is a good example? Which example worked best? How could that example be improved? What did you learn from that quiz? What are the best procedures for revising?

Actions. The instructor needs to demonstrate that he or she is actually learning from students' responses to improve the course. Emphasize what assignments are supposed to achieve and how students can evaluate those assignments in terms of their performance. Look for ways that you can improve the design of the course, with better exercises, effective use of class time, and rapid feedback. Don't try to masticate the subject into simple parts and be clearer, helpful, and so on, but devise situations that enable students to use their own devices to learn more effectively. Seek ways to demonstrate improvement, using grades and grade distributions as tools for evaluating effectiveness. Employ histograms to illustrate variance in performance. Employ run charts to show changes over time or to isolate problems with special causes.

Quality Team Actions. Conduct focus groups on isolated problems, create scattergrams correlating grades with other variables such as time on task, team effectiveness, and example effectiveness.

Stage 4: Reflective. Students offer ideas on better uses of class time, how to deal with questions, how to develop examples, use of tools such as concept maps, diagrams, and so on, and more challenging and interesting assignments. They search for ways to relate course material to previous experience and knowledge. The strategy of these responses is to become autonomous self-coaching learners.

Listening Focus. Try to learn how students make meaning out of your assignments. What are the reasoning sources of their errors? Focus on errors as sources of learning. How does past knowledge cause errors? Treat the students as colleagues and coproducers of learning, emphasizing their contributions to and responsibilities to learning in the course.

Actions. Attempt to make the reasoning and theories of learning applied in the course more transparent. This is why I devised the assignment; this is what I expected to happen. Turn suggestions and complaints back to the students: Why did you react that way? What were you thinking? What could you do to make this better? Incorporate what you learn into improved assignments. Document the improvements.

Quality Team Actions. Summarize what has been criticized and changed in the course. Offer overall suggestions for redesign and improvement, leading a discussion with the entire class. Teams should meet with instructor for debriefing.

Throughout this process, the quality team has moved from simply relaying complaints to being a model and partner in learning with both their classmates and the instructor. The team is the first to display the critical reflection because they are closest to its source: the instructor. Eventually, however, the goal is to have the whole class operating as a quality team.

Parkersburg was so convinced that quality improvement efforts belonged in the classroom that he struggled through the stages of student criticism with a battered ego but a heightened sense that successful learning required a partnership between instructor and learner. He now knows that learning is more complex than tell-and-test accounts and that to help someone learn demands all the intelligence, knowledge, and close observation he can manage. He also knows that he does not have to do this all alone. He can enlist the help of the learners individually, as quality teams, and as a whole class and guide them to being more critically reflective at the same time.

Since beginning to take learning and the criticism from learners seriously, Parkersburg no longer hums Ricky Nelson's anthem. He listens with care but no longer tries to please everyone. And no longer does he carry the burden of learning on his shoulders alone. No longer a frustrated rock star or stand-up comic, his vision of the instructor's work is more that of a producer-director of spectacular stories and dramas like Steven Spielberg. Every semester he still tells his new students, "Criticism is one of the most difficult but helpful intellectual skills that you will ever master." At the end of the semester, many of them believe it.

Reference

Angelo, T. A., and Cross, K. P. *Classroom Assessment Techniques: A Handbook for College Teachers*. (2nd ed.) San Francisco: Jossey-Bass, 1993.

LARRY SPENCE *is director of undergraduate learning initiatives, School of Information Sciences and Technology at The Pennsylvania State University.*

LISA FIRING LENZE *is former associate director of the Schreyer Institute for Innovation in Learning, The Pennsylvania State University.*

7

Focus groups are used frequently to gather information that is more robust than that which can be obtained by questionnaires. Contrary to popular opinion, this process can be done efficiently and used to gather useful feedback for the improvement of teaching.

Making Sense and Making Use of Feedback from Focus Groups

Richard Tiberius

Despite the increasing popularity of focus groups as a research tool in business, public life, and academe, many teachers have the impression that gathering feedback from focus groups is a frustrating and time-consuming process. No one wants to struggle with a ten-page transcript of student ramblings about her or his teaching, but no one should have to. Focus groups, administered properly, can produce highly useful feedback for teachers at a reasonable cost in time and effort. They should be as easy to administer and interpret as student ratings. Moreover, for improving certain aspects of teaching, focus groups are superior to written methods.

The comparison of written evaluations with focus groups is instructive. Today, the design and administration of student evaluations is a highly developed art. Principles of good design help designers write questionnaires that produce valid, reliable, and useful information (see, for example, Cashin, 1990, and the article "Making Sense of Student Written Comments" in this volume). However, not long ago, student questionnaires were frequently a source of frustration to teachers. Typically, several questions would be packed into a single item so that the teacher had no idea what a student's answer meant. Terms were often vague or abstract (for example, "Is the teacher effective?"). Other items were ambiguous. Teachers did not know what to make of students who "very strongly agreed" that "the teacher gives examples." Were students trying to say that the teacher gave too many examples or just enough? Clearly, questionnaire data are not inherently free of problems of interpretation, and solutions have been developed to overcome the problems. The problems of interpretation of focus group data also can be overcome by use of the proper methods.

Beginning with the Right Question

It is too late to start thinking about interpretation of the data when you are staring at a ten-page transcript of the rambling thoughts of a focus group. The process of focusing the respondent and sifting the information should begin much earlier. The place to begin is in the selection of the question or questions. The word focus in focus group evaluation needs to be taken seriously. A focus group discussion seems like a conversation, but its aim is not social. It is guided by a question or a few questions. Before you ask a colleague or teaching consultant to conduct a focus group in your behalf, you will need to work with the consultant to specify what information you want.

There are several sources of questions. The results of a written evaluation can form the stimulus for a focus group. The focus group follows up leads that were uncovered in the questionnaire. For example, if you learned from a student questionnaire that an uncomfortably large percentage of your students found the tutorials "not very helpful" to their learning, a focus group may be a useful way to find out why the tutorials were so perceived. The leader would likely begin the focus group by presenting the survey results. If I were the leader, I would begin the focus group something like this: "We're puzzled by the large number of your classmates who indicated that the tutorials were not very helpful to their learning. Obviously, we want them to be helpful, or we wouldn't go through the trouble of organizing them. Could you help us understand why they might not be considered helpful and what we may be able to do to improve them?"

Another common stimulus for focus groups is the need to reconcile contradictory feedback received from student ratings. I recall a botany teacher who asked me to run a focus group because his evaluations indicated that although half of the students indicated that his lectures were "highly organized," the other half complained that they were poorly organized. The questionnaire had flagged the issue of organization but did not help the teacher decide what to do. A focus group was organized to resolve the contradiction. What emerged from the discussion was a recognition that there were two groups of students: those who had previously taken a botany course perceived his lecture as disorganized, and those who were new to botany saw him as organized. On further discussion, it became clear that his use of a morphological classification was in conflict with the phylogenetic approach of the teacher who taught one of the prerequisite courses. The problem was addressed by his helping to translate between the two systems of classification for students who had taken the previous course.

Focus groups are useful not only for pursuing leads uncovered in questionnaires but also for generating the questionnaire items. Some of the best teachers find themselves short of good questions to ask. They would like to improve their teaching, but the standard questionnaire that they have been using has not revealed any particular problems. "No one is perfect," one teacher told me. "I'm sure there are things I could be working on if I knew what they were." I agreed with her that subtle aspects of teaching often elude the questionnaire. I told her that I could conduct a fishing expedition. I asked the group if they could help this very deserving teacher. I told them that "she generally receives excellent ratings on her questionnaires but would like to find areas in which she could make her course even better. Let's try to come up with something." It is always amazing to me how fertile a group like this can be.

Sometimes teachers know exactly what question they would like to ask but realize that students may not be able to answer it. One teacher wanted to know why students did not seem to like her. Attendance in her class was poor compared to other sections of the same course. She was not paranoid: the open-ended sections of her questionnaires were peppered with comments like "Dracula," and "frightening." She maintained that her standards were no higher than the other section teachers and her students' grades were no lower. What was the cause of the negative perception? Her evaluations contained lots of room for comments at the end, but students wrote no more than cryptic one-liners. We decided to conduct a focus group.

The purpose of the focus group was not to clarify or formulate the question but to help her students formulate their responses to the question. I invited the focus group to address her unpopularity directly. As I expected, at first they denied that she was unpopular. Then I mentioned the comments on the questionnaire, the rumors, and the poor attendance. After admitting that some students found the teacher frightening, they began rather timidly to address the topic. Once they got started, they talked for over forty minutes. There was a dramatic transition across the discussion. At first, students made snide comments that obliquely referred to her frightening image. My perception is that they were not trying to be evasive or cruel; they simply had not thought about the issue in sufficient depth to be capable of articulating their vague feelings. I listened to their remarks sympathetically but impassively, then asked for some examples. The examples helped others to attempt concepts that were closer to the mark, and those concepts stimulated further examples. Eventually, I was able to put together a descriptive paragraph that sounded accurate to most of them.

Thus, the first step toward achieving interpretable data from focus groups is to begin with the right kind of question. As my examples indicate, the best question is usually not the type that requires a specific answer. It is more like the statement of a problem that requires exploration by the group. The group leader puts her or his cards on the table by presenting a contradiction, a dilemma, a puzzle, or a concern to the focus group and asks the group to help the teacher understand it. The posture of the leader is characterized by the following sentences: "Here is something that has concerned your teachers. Can you help them?"

I cannot overemphasize the point about the importance of presenting the group with an issue in the proper context rather than asking a line of probing, specific questions. A negative example has reinforced this point for me. Course coordinators were disappointed because their students performed poorly on the exam, although they had put a great deal of effort into improving the course. They told me that they were certain that the course had been greatly improved by the reforms. They pointed to the student ratings that were consistently high, so whatever was the cause of the low performance, it was certainly not captured by any of the many items on their questionnaire.

I conducted a focus group to uncover the cause of the low performance, but it nearly failed because I had begun with a specific question that turned out to be the wrong one. I had asked the group for suggestions toward improving the course. They could think of none. At the end of the agreed-on time, as students were getting up from the table to leave, one of them said, "It would help if we had studied." I asked them all if they would sit down again for five minutes to follow up on this comment. It turned out that the course was so well organized and presented that they could afford to cram the night before the exam, leaving the majority of their study time for courses that were poorly taught. In retrospect, I should not have asked them how to improve the course; that question was too narrow to capture the real problem. The question that I should have put to the group was, "Your teachers are puzzled. Your class has indicated on the questionnaire that they find the course greatly improved, yet exam performance has not improved. Why is this?"

I would predict that this sort of general question would not work very well on a questionnaire because each student might give excuses for his or her own poor performance on the exam. But as a group, I would think that they would be more comfortable admitting that they were using a survival strategy. The question was more than a probe. It was an invitation to engage in dialogue in order to elicit the students' cooperation by providing them with an understanding of the teaching problem.

Summarizing and Gathering Examples and Anecdotes

I admit that I have presented questions that help me make the point about the critical role of the question in facilitating the interpretation of focus group discussion. Perhaps it is not surprising that if you present a problem to the group, that is what they will address. And if you convene the focus group to find out why students have negative feelings about a teacher, you will not need an elaborate coding system to find that the main theme of the transcript will be student feelings about the teacher. But asking the right question is only the beginning. The right question may focus the discussion, but forty minutes worth of focused discussion may still be overwhelming. The discussion must be boiled down. Themes, issues, or ideas must be succinctly stated. The place to begin doing this is during the focus group, not with ten pages of transcript from a group session. The focus group leader uses the summary, one of the most powerful tools in the toolbox of the small group leader, to clarify the important points. At certain points in the discussion, the group leader summarizes the point that students appear to be making and asks them to correct the summary if it does not yet capture their thoughts.

This corrective process facilitates the interpretation of issues and is essential to the understanding of subtle issues. Students are often incapable of articulating subtle issues clearly. My guess is that they simply have not given much thought to the issue raised by the group leader. The iterative process is a way of helping them reflect. Let us return to the example of the teacher who wanted to investigate her unpopularity.

Early in the discussion, there was little to summarize since their comments were not very descriptive. They were functioning at what I call the name-calling stage. But students soon tire of name calling, especially when the group leader is gently reminding them that the goal is to write something helpful to the teacher. I asked them to be more specific, to give examples. Their examples and stories were the stimulus for further thinking. For example, one student said, "She fires questions at us." Another qualified, "It's not the pace of the questions; it's that you feel stupid if you can't answer them." These examples allowed another student to risk an interpretive statement: "It's basically that she assumes we know more than we do." At this point, I probed a little: "Is the course pitched at too high a level?" Their responses clearly indicated that this was not the case; the level of the course was fine. The readings were not difficult to understand, and the exam was appropriate. The problem was becoming clearer: it had something to do with an intimidating teaching style, particularly with forcing people to answer questions in front of the entire class.

This process of exemplifying, summarizing, and correcting continues until the group is reasonably satisfied with my summary of their perceptions. If there is time, I encourage the group to explore ways to overcome the problem. The danger inherent in the use of the summary is that it might communicate to the class a hidden agenda to achieve a consensus. I counter this assumption by stating clearly to the group that I am interested not in establishing consensus but in uncovering the range of opinions on each issue. However, this is a technical matter for the skilled focus group leader.

The Issue of Transcribing

Readers who are familiar with focus group research may expect me to recommend transcription and analysis of the focus group discussion. If you were gathering information as part of a classroom research project or using the data for evidence of teaching excellence, you might want to go to the expense of transcribing the entire discussion. I will return to the subject of developing a code for such rigorous analysis. For the purpose of improving teaching, the judicious use of questioning and summarizing techniques should enable the group leader to produce a few paragraphs that capture the key points of the group. These can be typed out or dictated by the group leader while he or she is listening to the audiotape. If the summaries have been sufficiently clear, I may not even use videotape. I dictate or type the summaries when I get back to the office based on notes made during the focus group. When I do this, I find that unless I have captured some of the examples, my summary is dry and abstract. I have to go back in my notes to find the rich examples.

Communicating to the Teacher

Now I would like to revise that off-putting image of the ten-page discursive transcript of a focus group discussion that we imagined on a teacher's desk. In its place are two or three pages summarizing the key themes, ideas, or issues, plus recommendations, all supported by quotations from students in their own colorful language. What does a teacher do with this brief report? Sometimes the report is sufficiently rich to speak for itself; in the first example that follows, the teacher understood the feedback and was able to take remedial action after reading the report. Other times it is a stimulus for further exploration and reflection, as in the second example: the teacher understood the feedback but did not know what actions to take as a result. The feedback was a stimulus for further inquiry. For a third group of teachers, the report by itself is insufficient. Such teachers develop an understanding of the issues only after an extensive dialogue with the focus group leader or even directly with the students themselves. Following are excerpts from various consultation reports that I have sent to teachers summarizing the results of a focus group. These illustrate the three situations.

The following excerpt provided a sufficiently rich source of information to have an impact on the teacher. It focused on one aspect of teaching and provided detailed feedback about the problem and even remedies.

The Main Weakness of the Course

There is no doubt that the main difficulty students are having with your course is the lack of a clear set of learning objectives. They are not sure what they are expected to know at the end of each lecture, what they are expected to take away from a case, what they are supposed to take away from the course, or what they will be asked to do for the essay.

"There is no structure, no guidelines."
"There is no final, bottom line."
"It's not organized."
"There's no logical flow."
"The lecture needs to be smoother, to have a beginning, middle and end."

The group discussed a number of explanations for this lack of direction. These explanations are interrelated in complex ways. I will try to organize them as clearly as I can, although they were completely mixed up in the free-flowing discussion.

Lecturing. Lecturing was the focus of their conversation about lack of direction. It was not surprising to me that they focused on the lecture. After all, it is to the lectures that students traditionally turn for help in understanding difficult concepts and for the goals of the course. They have difficulty following your lecture. They don't see the logical flow. The thoughts seem "fragmented" or "scattered."

The problem is further clarified in the suggestions that they made for improvement: provide clear learning objectives of each class. Knowing what they are expected to take away from each class would help them focus their attention during class and help them focus their study efforts afterward.

Summing Up. They would like to see you sum up the main point after interacting with students and before moving on to another topic. As much as they appreciate your listening carefully to their views, they want to know what you think too. You have the expert knowledge that they desire. They believe that you have important wisdom to convey that is not wholly conveyed through the rather spotty interaction with students.

As one student put it, "He's too nice a guy. He listens to everyone and accepts everyone's ideas, but we are left not knowing where he stands." The student went on to say that students don't want arrogant teachers, but humility can go too far if it means that "we are not hearing his ideas." Another student appreciates the group participation but would like to see you sum things up at the end. A third student said that you should expand on the points that students make in class rather than simply accept them: "We don't know his viewpoints," added this student.

Others argued that a summary of the main points just prior to the case would help them apply the concepts to the case.

Provide Handouts. A few students argued that they would appreciate handouts of the major ideas, concepts, or at least the learning objectives. Again, the context of this suggestion is an inability to understand the lecture.

Overheads. The experts on media tell us that overheads are supposed to provide brief retrieval cues or memory joggers. They are not supposed to substitute for a coherent flow of prose. The fact that students complained that your overheads are too fragmentary indicates that they were seeking, in the overheads, an alternate route to understanding the material. Again, the problem is not with the overheads themselves but with the coherency of the lecture itself:

"The overheads are more a pointer for himself. They are not helpful to us."
"They are not linked to the material."
"He should give the overheads to someone to edit them."
"I copied them down and grammatically they don't make sense."
"He shouldn't read the overhead. He's much better when he speaks freely."
"I would rather have no overheads if he is just going to read them."

Why? The group volunteered explanations for the lack of organization in the lectures. I found these revealing. Although the students are deeply troubled by not having a clear focus for their learning, they appear to have a respectful and understanding attitude toward you:

"He knows so much that it is difficult for him to talk at our level."
"He is thinking about so many complex things that he forgets to say the
    obvious."
"He has seen forty cases like this, and we have just seen one, so it's difficult
    for him to relate to what we see, or don't see, in the case."
"He assumes that we have a lot of background that we don't have."
"He doesn't want to take control."

The teacher was enormously encouraged by this feedback. Despite its critical message, the tone was supportive and affectionate toward the teacher. Prior to the focus group, his attitude toward the students had been angry and negative. Based on previous student evaluations, he had developed a view of the students as punitive and arbitrary. The focus group was a turning point. After reading the rich descriptive paragraphs in the students' own words, he realized that the students liked him and empathized with his situation. What they wanted was entirely reasonable: a few technical changes that he was quite capable of delivering, not a change in his personality.

The second excerpt is a descriptive paragraph about a teacher's persona that stimulated her to explore her teaching behavior more systematically.

Your Persona

In the perceptions of these students, your persona is highly favorable. They saw you as "a very good person," "a good professor," "considerate of the students," "not arrogant," and "the kind of teacher who doesn't embarrass students." They view you as treating students in a manner that indicates respect for the students.

This perception of you is based largely on the interaction that you have with students in class. They perceive you as listening well, interested in students, and accepting of their views.

But please repeat students' questions and answers. The interaction could be further enhanced if you would repeat the questions asked by students and answers given by students, especially students in the front row, who cannot be heard at the back. Students pointed out that you do repeat the answers sometimes, but not always.

The teacher was gratified to learn that the class was aware of her caring attitude toward them. She always thought of herself as a person who cares for her students, but she had no idea that her students appreciated her attitude. She was interested in finding out specifically what it is that she does in the class to convey her caring attitude. In Donald Schön's (1983) words, she wanted to gain awareness of her teaching through reflection. She asked if her teaching could be videotaped so that she could observe herself. She disclosed that in one of her other classes, students did not perceive her in such a flattering light, and she wanted to compare herself in the two classes. Was she more relaxed in one class? Did she like one group of students better? She was surprised to hear that students in her class could not hear the questions of other students. She wondered whether there were other things like this that were responsible for her negative image in the other class.

The third excerpt is taken from the report of the teacher who wanted to know why she seemed to frighten students. I put together a descriptive paragraph that sounded accurate to most of them, and this paragraph was supported by a few student quotations.

Pinpointing Students

The students use an expression, pinpointing, which refers to the strategy of asking questions of specific students rather than asking general questions of the class. They believe that this strategy, more than anything else, is responsible for the unsafe atmosphere in the class:

"No one likes feeling stupid in front of the whole class."

"It's not easy to think on your feet."

"You may be far away, you know, just for that minute, even though you generally were paying attention, and then 'zap,' you're hit with this question, like, 'What did I do?'"

The teacher attended to every paragraph in the report except this one. When I drew it to her attention, she waved it off. "I don't know what they mean," she said, "but it can't be that I frighten them." Her self-image strongly contradicted the perceptions of the students. She referred to herself as a new faculty member, small in stature, with a weak, high-pitched voice. Then she giggled, "Who am I frightening?" I remembered that the students were serious about their opinions regarding the cause of the fearsome atmosphere, so I pressed a little further, but she refused to consider it. Finally, I suggested that she might benefit from a face-to-face discussion with students. I explained to her that face-to-face meetings often allow teachers to understand emotional meanings that are lost in the report. The actual meeting is described in the next section.

Face-to-Face Conversation

Face-to-face conversation between teacher and students is an excellent tool for interpreting information from the focus group that does not pop off the pages, such as the emotional tone of messages. The challenge is to create a safe group climate so that the discussion will be frank and constructive. In the face-to-face group, radical or destructive comments by individuals with extreme views can be hurtful and may stifle the conversation. In contrast, the summarizing and checking process used in the focus group eliminates extreme views. Members of a face-to-face group need to be chosen carefully with the group atmosphere in mind. For this reason, I usually choose volunteers from the class who are willing to spend an hour with the teacher to help her develop constructive responses to the student feedback. Such a blatantly cooperative agenda is usually a sufficient disincentive to weed out the snipers.

Our teacher put her question to the students directly. She could not suppress a laugh as she made the point that students in the focus group had found her technique of pinpointing students intimidating. She expected that this issue would be washed out in a gale of laughter. She was taken aback by the stony faces. When she recovered, she stated, as if it were the final proof of the silliness of this issue, that whenever there were no volunteers to answer her question, she would revise the question, making it easier. "So how can you lose?" she added. After a long silence, one student quietly suggested that making the question easier raises the stakes. "If you think it's humiliating to answer a tough question, it's much more so if you blow a question that's been made easier." After the group left, she disclosed to me that she would have never realized the extent to which this apparently innocent game troubled her students if she had not witnessed their expressions first hand.

Coding the Transcript for Research

You may have noticed that I have avoided the usual rigorous and systematic analysis of focus group transcripts. I wanted to deliver on my promise that focus groups, administered properly, can produce highly useful feedback for teachers at a reasonable cost in time and effort. For the purpose of improving teaching, the analysis of focus group data does not have to be more rigorous than I have described. The validation of the data lies in the continuation of the process: further explorations of teaching, other methods of gathering feedback, implementation of the suggestions. The teacher whose course lacked clear learning objectives may have missed some subtle aspects of the focus group discussion because they were not picked up by the crude method of creating the summary report, but he surely did not miss the students' main issue. We would expect students to be happier with his teaching after he responds to this issue. If they are not, we can conduct another focus group.

The teacher who became interested in videotaping her classes to find out why her students in one class perceived her as caring developed a hypothesis about the difference between these students and students in another class. She believed that the distinction between the two classes was explained by a "caring versus uncaring" dimension. After viewing video-tapes and perhaps conducting interviews or administering more question-naires, she may discover that the concept of caring is not precisely the distinction between the two classes. She may find out that the distinction between the two classes is not between caring and uncaring but between caring and unenthusiastic, or some other dimension. She may then begin to examine the causes of their perception of her lack of enthusiasm for the course. The focus group provided her with a starting point. It raised her awareness of an important variable. My experience with the path of teaching improvement is that the process begins when a teacher has a powerful insight, and then it quickly diverges into unpredictable directions that are usually fruitful.

That said, there is a place for the rigorous analysis of the transcript—for example, in classroom research and documentation of teaching for promotion. Let us stay with the example of the teacher whose students in one class perceived her as caring. Assume further that she wanted to conduct a classroom research project to find out if caring was in fact the missing element in the other class that did not perceive her as favorably. Her research design requires that she change her teaching in predictable ways and then measure the effects of those changes using several focus groups. What she needs to know from the transcripts is whether the dimension "caring-uncaring" is supported more than, say "enthusiasm-lack of enthusiasm" or some other dimensions that may be more important for that group. In this research situation, we are looking not for a red flag to stimulate action whose impact can be evaluated later; rather, we are attempting to discriminate between competing hypotheses. For the latter purpose, we need to search every sentence, or "thought unit," or word of the transcript for evidence to support one or the other hypothesis. Moreover, the researchers need to be particularly fastidious about searching for evidence to disconfirm their hypothesis. They must attempt to find every scrap of evidence to support the competing hypothesis that the second class is less concerned with caring than it is with some other dimension. This process may lead the researchers to count and contrast the number of statements made about caring in the focus groups taken from the two different classes. The precise method for doing this is in Miles and Huberman (1994). Having developed a theory, the researchers may run follow-up focus groups to test the theory in the manner of grounded theory (Corbin and Strauss, 1990).

When to Use Focus Groups

I have intentionally painted a rosy picture of focus groups to counter the prevailing prejudice that they are not worth the trouble. I would like to encourage you to try this powerful method of gathering information to improve your teaching. On the other hand, I feel obligated to end with a realistic assessment of its strengths and weaknesses. The process that I have described here requires about eight hours of the consultant's time and about three hours of the teacher's time (for a more detailed explanation, see Tiberius, Sackin, Janzen, and Preece, 1993). It is not procedure in which to engage routinely. Following are the conditions in which I have found the time well worth it:

- When you do not understand the feedback from a questionnaire or have contradictory feedback from a questionnaire and want to follow it up with a focus group. Two examples were given in this article: one of a teacher who received feedback that the tutorials were not very helpful to his students' learning and another of a teacher who received contradictory feedback about the organization of his lectures.
- When you do not know what to ask and you use the focus group to fish for ideas. An example was given in this article of a teacher who always received complimentary feedback on her student questionnaires but was concerned that the questionnaires were not asking the right questions.
- When students do not know how to articulate feedback and the focus group can be used to formulate their opinions. In one of the examples, the teacher was intimidating her students; at least, that is what she understood from her questionnaires. The focus group helped students specify the origin of their negative feelings.
- When you do not seem to understand what the problem is. A focus group led by the teacher can help. The teacher who was intimidating her students found it difficult to accept until she talked with the students in a face-to-face meeting.
- When you want to ensure the acceptability of a new teaching method. When teachers and consultants devise teaching interventions in response to feedback from students, they cannot be sure that these methods are acceptable to students. The focus group members can be asked to give their opinions on the acceptability of the suggested methods.
- When there is a need to clarify subtle issues or complex issues involving multiple variables. Relationship issues in particular are well served by the use of focus groups. For example, students rarely express issues of trust, respect, responsibility, or safety on a questionnaire, and yet these are known to be important dimensions (Tiberius and Billson, 1991) for students.
- When delivering amplifying feedback as opposed to corrective feedback. When most teachers think about feedback, they mean corrective feedback, meaning information from students that identifies a poor teaching performance such as illegible print size on the overheads. The teacher can then "correct" this error by increasing the print size. Questionnaires are efficient at identifying such errors in performance. But other ways of improving teaching do not involve ways that teachers can correct their performances but ways that teachers can become made more effective by enhancing something that they are already doing. For example, the teacher may create a more positive attitude in the class by building an alliance with

the learners (see Tiberius and Billson, 1991). Interventions of the amplifying kind are not simply a matter of doing more of this or less of that. They are not one- or two-dimensional, and therefore they require a deep understanding of the situation before a teacher knows what to do.

References

Cashin, W. E. "Student Ratings of Teaching: Recommendations for Use." (IDEA paper no. 22.) Manhattan: Kansas State University, Center for Faculty Evaluation and Development, 1990.

Corbin, J., and Strauss, A. *Basics of Qualitative Research: Grounded Theory Procedures and Techniques.* Thousand Oaks, Calif.: Sage, 1990.

Miles, M. B., and Huberman, A. M. *Qualitative Data Analysis.* (2nd ed.) Thousand Oaks, Calif.: Sage, 1994.

Schön, D. A. *The Reflective Practitioner: How Professionals Think in Action.* New York: Basic Books, 1983.

Tiberius, R. G., and Billson, J. M. (eds.). *The Social Context of Teaching and Learning.* New Directions for Teaching and Learning, no. 45. San Francisco: Jossey-Bass, 1991.

Tiberius, R. G., Sackin, H. D., Janzen, K. R., and Preece, M. "Alliances for Change: A Procedure for Improving Teaching Through Conversations with Learners and Partnerships with Colleagues." *Journal of Staff, Program, and Organization Development,* 1993, *11,* 11–23.

RICHARD TIBERIUS is director of the Centre for Research in Education and professor in the Department of Psychiatry at the University of Toronto, Canada.

8

*What can you do if none of the teaching assessment
instruments addresses the questions you have about your
teaching and your students' learning? Some suggestions
for creating your own questions that target your needs
and interests are given.*

Writing Teaching Assessment Questions for Precision and Reflection

William L. Rando

Despite the proliferation of teaching assessment instruments and teaching consultants to assist in the process, faculty members may still want to write their own teaching assessment questions. The challenge is to ask the best possible questions in the best possible way.

Types of Questions

In this article, I distinguish questions in two different ways: self-report and direct assessment questions. Self-report questions are the kind we most often think about when considering assessment. They ask students to rate, rank, report, or tell about some aspect of their learning experience. These questions may use Likert-type scales. The following questions are rated on a 5-point scale: Strongly Disagree, Disagree, Not Applicable, Agree, Strongly Disagree:

1. Students are invited to contribute ideas in class.
2. Instructor communicates ideas clearly.
3. I learned a lot in this course.
4. I think I am meeting the objectives of this course.

   Self-report questions can also be more open and descriptive:

1. In what ways does the class discussion help you achieve your goals for this course?

2. What additional types of feedback would help you achieve your goals for this course?
3. In what ways could this assignment/test/lecture be improved?

The other type of assessment question is a direct assessment of student learning. These questions ask students to show what they know or how they know it. They are similar to the questions asked on tests and quizzes, but are used here to assess the quality of instruction and its impact on student learning at any point during the course:

Before a lecture: "Take a moment to think about yesterday's lecture, and describe two threats to validity in the study we discussed."
During a break in the lecture: "Think about the process I just described. Now look at the chart on page 200, and tell me whether you think growth will continue at the same rate, slow down, or accelerate."
After a lecture: "Today I talked about two theories of decision making. Think about a decision you've made recently and describe it in the terms of each theory" or "What is the most important idea you learned in today's lecture?"

The second decision to make is between open-ended and closed-ended assessment questions. Open-ended questions are designed to explore students' experiences or the broadest objectives of our teaching. An excellent example of an open-ended question is the one-minute paper, which asks, "What's the most important thing you learned and what question are you left with?" (Angelo and Cross, 1993). These questions provide minimal limitations on students' responses, resulting in valuable feedback on what students are really experiencing. The examples self-report questions are open-ended.

Closed-ended questions provide answers to specific questions about students' experiences and learning. For example, after lecturing on two theoretical approaches to the study of aging, I may want to see if my students can make distinctions based on examples. For this, a closed-ended assessment question would work well. The Likert-type examples already given are of this type. Since closed-ended questions typically require shorter responses, we can use them in groups of three, five, ten, or more.

These types of questions can be combined to form the simple two-by-two grid shown in Figure 8.1:

Quadrant A: Open-ended, self-report questions for exploring students' experiences
Quadrant B: Closed-ended, self-report questions for identifying specific aspects of students' learning experiences.
Quadrant C: Open-ended, direct assessment questions for exploring what students are learning in a general way

Figure 8.1. Question Type Choice Grid

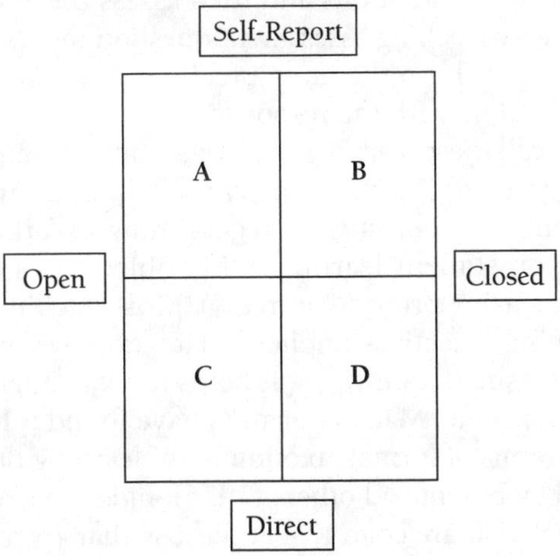

```
              Self-Report
        ┌──────────┬──────────┐
        │          │          │
        │    A     │    B     │
┌──────┐│          │          │┌────────┐
│ Open ││          │          ││ Closed │
└──────┘│          │          │└────────┘
        │    C     │    D     │
        │          │          │
        └──────────┴──────────┘
              Direct
```

Quadrant D: Closed-ended, direct assessment questions to identify specific areas of understanding, confusion and learning

Guidelines for Writing Questions

There is something of an art to writing questions for surveys, but you can use some common sense to identify the areas in which questions will be most useful for you. If you are going to go to the trouble of gathering student data, a little extra time thinking about the key questions can save you confusion and time in interpretation later.

Ask Questions That Will Produce Responses You Can Use. This may seem obvious, but it is the most often mentioned criticism leveled against standardized feedback questions, exemplified by the following comment: "These results don't mean anything to me." Even given the chance to write our own questions, it is easy to fall back on familiar questions—for example, "Rate the quality of this class" or "What did you like best about this section?" These questions are probably too vague to be of help to anyone, but even if they are well crafted, specific responses can be unhelpful if they do not speak to the particular instructor's way of teaching. For example, questions that ask students to comment on the instructor's presentation style do not do much for an instructor who relies on the discussion method. Similarly, assessment questions about the amount of material covered may not be helpful to an instructor whose primary goal is for students to develop critical thinking skills. The key to writing assessment questions that will produce useful responses is to base questions on specific objectives for student learning.

Learning objectives are precise statements of the changes we are trying to create in our students. When we ask ourselves how we expect students to be different as a result of our teaching, we can construct questions that truly speak to our core intentions and then assess the effects of the methods we choose. Every teaching assessment question relates to what we hope our students accomplish, so the more precise we are about objectives, the more pleased we will be with the responses.

Notice that I call these learning objectives, not teaching objectives. The key to exploiting our objectives effectively is in shifting focus from the teaching of content ("My objective is to get through World War I by Thursday") to a focus on student learning ("My objective is to help students develop arguments using primary sources"). Most teaching professors proffer multiple learning objectives implicitly. However, when we are trying to write effective assessment questions, it helps to make these implicit objectives explicit and specific. Many educators have found it helpful to look at their teaching in terms of formal taxonomies of learning objectives, such as the one proposed by Bloom and others (1956). Bloom makes the distinction between objectives that are cognitive and those that are affective. We consider only the cognitive taxonomy, which starts with knowledge (factual information that form the basis for reasoning) and ends with evaluation (judgments based on facts and intellectual operations that make up the center of the taxonomy):

Knowledge (the acquisition of facts)
Comprehension (explaining complex systems, ideas, and processes)
Application (using ideas in new contexts)
Analysis (taking ideas and processes apart)
Synthesis (combining ideas to form new ideas)
Evaluation (judging the quality, value, fit, or validity of ideas and processes)

It is not necessary to use Bloom or any other taxonomy to articulate learning objectives, but many educators find it useful. The important thing is to figure out what we want our students to do and to write questions that will produce responses that speak to that goal. Following are four questions (one from each sector of the grid and so labeled) used by a faculty member whose objective is to teach the application of theory to practice using case studies:

"How did analyzing case studies help you prepare for the final project?" [sector A]
"Analyzing cases taught me to apply theory to practice." [This is followed by a 5-point scale from Definitely No to Definitely Yes; sector B]
"Apply theory A to the following situation, and write a paragraph on your conclusions." [sector C]
"According to theory A, which of the following is true about the paragraph you just read? (a) Workers are unmotivated. (b) Workers are underprepared. (c) Workers are over qualified." [sector D]

Each of these questions will produce markedly different responses, each one valuable in its own way. The sector A question can be used to explore students' experiences with cases and to determine if students can articulate the value of analyzing cases. The sector B question would probably be asked in a group of other specific questions and would elicit detailed but limited responses and an idea of how widespread the response was among the students. The sector C question could assess students' general abilities to apply theory to practice, a direct measure of our objective. And the sector D question, like the sector B question, would probably be one of many questions that produce specific insights into students' skills and the spread of responses.

Ask Questions That Are Reflective Opportunities for Students. Assessment questions to induce reflection in students are useful for two reasons. First, if students start thinking deeply about their learning experiences, their replies are more likely to be valuable and insightful. Ask questions superficially, and students may reply in kind. The rule here is to ask for what you want. If you want to find out how a lecture, assignment, or activity has helped students learn, then ask the whole question, including your goals for the assignment:

"The assignment you just completed was designed to give you practice turning unformed data into specific, answerable questions. Take a look at the random data below, organize them into a question, and describe the steps you took to develop that question." [sectors A and C]

"Today's lecture described the development of the city-state from two distinctly different perspectives. Thinking about our example, take five minutes and highlight the primary differences between these two perspectives." [sector C]

"Prior to last night's reading, I assigned three response questions that were designed to help you explore some of the implicit assumptions made by the author. In the light of the author's assumptions, what can you say about the limitations of her conclusions?" [sector C]

Although these are all direct assessment questions, they allow students to formulate content in the context of pedagogical goals, reflecting on what they know and how the teaching has helped them know it.

The second reason to think about assessment as an opportunity for student reflection is that when students reflect on how they learn, they become better learners. When students reflect on things that support or hinder learning, they hone their meta-cognitive capabilities; that is, they develop mental processes that help them manage information, identify confusion, and develop learning strategies. For instance, some students draw a diagram when words alone fail to produce understanding. Some students develop reading questions to enhance their comprehension of difficult texts. Some students study in groups or pairs to reinforce their understanding.

Unfortunately, other students have not developed their meta-cognitive skills, so they waste time studying and practicing in ways that do not help them learn. Asking students to reflect on the learning process after giving them an assignment or exercise gives them a chance to realize something about their own cognitive style. We enhance the quality of assessment questions, drawing students into the teaching-learning experience, when we describe our goals and methods in the question itself:

"Last night I assigned guided questions along with the reading. Think about how your understanding today differs from how you understood previous readings, and describe the difference, if any." [sector A]

"These three exercises were designed to improve your ability to analyze complex and unformed problems. Think about which activity was most helpful for you, and describe how it helps you." [sector A]

"In today's discussion, I asked questions in a new way. Describe your experience in today's discussion, and write a short paragraph on the question of what would have happened if there had been no battle at Gettysburg." [sectors A and C]

Ask Questions That Reveal Something to You About Teaching in Your Discipline or Area. Assessment questions can also contribute to the dialogue about teaching within a department or discipline. Individual disciplines, like individual instructors, have their own, often implicit, set of learning objectives and methods. Historians analyze primary texts, sociologists and anthropologists use ethnography and statistical analysis, teachers of literature do close readings and analysis of criticism, economists solve problems, and biologists have labs. Learning objectives and teaching methods reflect the research methods of the discipline, but they do not always mirror them completely. Other values, such as those embedded in our understanding of "liberal education," intervene, providing objectives that go beyond research skills. For instance, faculty members often include among their goals for students the development of citizenship skills, increased understanding of others, improved communication or human relation skills, and even spiritual development and social or economic advancement. These values sometimes drive dialogues about teaching within a discipline. Faculty members who have questions such as, "Does majoring in political science increase political involvement?" or "Does participation in sociology classes increase appreciation for persons from different groups?" or "Are problem sets really the best way to develop students' abilities to do economics?" can use assessment questions to make contributions to these dialogues.

For years, heads of schools of engineering believed that the best way to prepare engineers was to load students up with basic sciences for two and a half years and then allow them to focus on design work late in their junior year. Faculty members and researchers who began looking at their teaching from the perspective of the discipline have since begun to realize that design, not basic science, is the core of the engineering major and that introducing design concepts early in a student's course of study can increase retention in subsequent basic science and help retain students in the field. Sometimes the way that disciplines organize learning is not the best way, and assessment can be used to determine that. Consider the following assessment questions:

"The purpose of this course is to prepare you to do a major research proposal next semester. Describe the steps you will take to develop that proposal and your general sense of readiness to take those steps." [sectors A and C]
"This literature course is designed to provide intensive preparation in writing. Look at the items below, and place a check next to those that you feel you have mastered this semester." [sector B]
"This literature course is designed to provide intensive preparation in close reading. Read the poem below, and provide a one-page analysis of it." [sector D]
"In the past three years, each of your history courses has been preparing you to write a senior thesis. Looking back, which assignments, classroom activities, lectures, and discussions have done the most to prepare you?" [sector A]

Conclusion

We can add greater precision to teaching assessment questions by thinking about why we want to assess: Are we exploring students' experiences or collecting specific data on students' learning? We can elicit more powerful responses by asking questions that come from our specific learning objectives. We can create greater, more reflective responses from students by sharing the thinking behind our teaching and asking them to reflect specifically on their learning experience. And, finally, we may want to frame teaching questions in the context of developing knowledge about teaching in our discipline. In this way, we invite others, our colleagues in particular, into the conversation.

References

Angelo, T. A., and K. P. *Classroom Assessment Techniques: A Handbook for College Teachers*. (2nd ed.) San Francisco: Jossey-Bass, 1993.
Bloom, B. S., and others. *Taxonomy of Educational Objectives*. New York: McKay, 1956.

WILLIAM L. RANDO *is the director of the Teaching Fellow Preparation and Development Center at Yale University.*

9

Student ratings are one of the most widely used measures of teaching in education today. All users should understand what the numbers mean and how they should and should not be used.

Interpreting the Numbers: Using a Narrative to Help Others Read Student Evaluations of Your Teaching Accurately

Jennifer Franklin

Your academic livelihood or reputation may someday depend on how others interpret the evaluations your students have given you and your course. Like them or not, ratings are now in use in over 90 percent of all colleges and universities in the United States (Seldin, 1984) and are in widespread use by faculty committees and academic administrators such as deans and department chairs to make personnel decisions: merit review, promotion, and tenure for tenure-track faculty and hire-or-fire decisions for adjunct faculty. Submitting a well-written, well-reasoned narrative discussing your students' evaluations of your teaching (that is, ratings) is an opportunity to improve the odds that your reviewers will consider your students' opinions in the full context of the complex factors that shaped them. The reflection needed to write an effective narrative can help you in two important ways. The first is that you defend yourself from misuse of your ratings (and in doing so increase the incentive for academic decision makers to do a better job of using ratings for everyone). A narrative can help your reviewers gain a fuller understanding of ratings as a valuable but imperfect measure of teaching effectiveness and therefore help them avoid common misinterpretation and misuses of data that can adversely affect their evaluation of your teaching. A narrative can also remind colleagues that they, not your students, are the evaluators of record. Student evaluations are data for review by colleagues, not canned, ready-made evaluations on which to base personnel decisions.

NEW DIRECTIONS FOR TEACHING AND LEARNING, no. 87, Fall 2001 © John Wiley & Sons, Inc.

The second way that writing a narrative can help is to offer you insight that can help you improve your ratings by improving your teaching. Writing a ratings narrative can also benefit your own education and development as a scholar of teaching as a discipline as well as a scholar who teaches a discipline. Just as keeping a journal can foster reflective practice as a teacher, taking the time to consider and record what your student ratings mean to you can provide new insights into your teaching practices and your relationship with your students. The challenge is to convey the meaning and importance of your students' feedback at the same time you put your ratings data in perspective.

Although students have much valuable feedback to offer, including ratings when properly collected, do not assume that those who will examine these ratings have the necessary skills and knowledge to use them within guidelines recommended by ratings experts. There is too much evidence to the contrary. My colleague Michael Theall and I have conducted several studies over the past fifteen years examining what ratings users know about how ratings data should be used. In one multi-institutional study, more than half of the faculty using ratings of their colleagues could not answer basic questions about the common statistics that appear on typical ratings reports, such as means and standard deviations. Others were willing to use data substantially flawed by poor sampling within classes or across an instructor's teaching load simply because it was "better than no data" (Franklin and Theall, 1989; Theall and Franklin, in press). Our findings have given rise to the concerns and suggestions in this article.

Evaluate the Evaluation Process

Whatever purpose you have for constructing a narrative, understanding how student ratings in your campus's appraisal process compare with widely recognized standards for good practice can provide perspective. If your ratings are being used for personnel decisions, a narrative can explain why your ratings are really great or, if they are not, mitigate the damage they may cause. Understanding how ratings are supposed to work according to standards for good practice can serve you either way if you are able to articulate authoritatively why your ratings should or should not count in an evaluation of your teaching effectiveness.

The first premise of a well-constructed faculty evaluation plan is that teaching is a multidimensional enterprise—that is, that faculty have many roles as teachers: developing course content, planning courses and instructional activities, constructing course materials, presenting instructional information, assessing student learning, giving students instructional and motivational feedback, and, more recently, course Web developer, to name just some. The second premise is that there are potentially multiple sources of data concerning each role. Student feedback is only one such source and is not equally applicable to every role. Potential sources of data concerning the various dimensions of teaching include students, alumni, faculty who are content experts, faculty who are pedagogical experts, administrators such as department chairs, specialists such as faculty developers, instructional developers, evaluators, and, of course, the instructor being evaluated.

The more sources of data and the better matched they are to the dimension of teaching being considered, the better the overall plan is. For example, students are unlikely to be the best judges of the quality, currency, or accuracy of course content; expert colleagues in the field are. Thus, the widely used ratings items asking students to judge the expertise of a teacher are unlikely to provide the most valid data. However, compared with a visiting colleague untrained in systematic observation techniques who spends an hour and a half observing one class, students who spend an entire semester in a course are uniquely qualified to comment on the pace of the instruction, the classroom atmosphere, or whether difficult concepts are presented clearly. Arreola's excellent, practical guide to comprehensive faculty evaluations systems, Developing a Comprehensive Faculty Evaluation System (2000), can help assess the quality of a department's process.

The following factors are vital to get valid and reliable data about teaching performance from ratings:

Ratings questionnaires must be properly constructed and administered.
Ratings data must be summarized in formats that provide readers with essential information about response rates, frequencies, average or typical (mean or modal) response, information about the spread or dispersion of student responses, and, if possible, benchmarks based on a criterion or normative data.
Those who will use the data must have the information they need for analysis and interpretation using the reports as provided.
The interpretations and conclusions that result must be evaluated and applied in the context of a well-constructed, comprehensive, and effectively implemented system for evaluating teaching

There are a lot of qualifications and even hedges in these assertions, but in essence, if ratings are used properly, they can provide useful information about the quality of instruction students have received. In my experience, the greatest amount of care is put into the first step, and the rest is taken for granted. The resulting problem is that no matter how good the questionnaire was, if reviewers lack the needed skills and knowledge, the ratings are no more than a Rorschach test with numbers instead of inkblots. Readers will look at the report and imagine they see what they already believe, a fine conclusion if they are already convinced you are a fabulous teacher, but what if they are not so inclined? Your narrative is an opportunity to put

some objectivity back into the numbers by raising questions about the context of the data being considered.

The Most Common Ratings Problems

To get the most effect from your narrative, you should be prepared to identify and address the most common and potentially harmful types of errors
in ratings: misuse of data, bad data, and misinterpretation of ratings.

Even your best effort might not outweigh strongly entrenched bad faculty evaluation practices, but the efforts you make in this direction will at
least be preparation should you need to explore legal remedies if you are
harmed by those practices. Even if your ratings are less than optimum, standards for good practice in ratings use are similar to standards for due
process. In a fair personnel action, bad, misused, or misinterpreted data cannot be used against you.

Misuse of Ratings Data. Student ratings are all too frequently given
undue weight in judging teaching effectiveness. To understand the problem
of overreliance on ratings data, first consider a probable source of the problem. Finding the best available match between a dimension of teaching and
the best available data is often a challenge. Some otherwise good sources,
such as multiple, trained observers coming to your classroom several times,
may not be affordable or available. Overreliance may also result from a ten-
dency to view numbers as more objective and possibly less subject to dispute
than more qualitative approaches. Peer evaluation is often avoided lest it
strain collegiality. Whatever the cause, if ratings are overused at your institution, keeping a teaching portfolio that also includes a narrative analysis of
your ratings can offer you an opportunity to inject more data in the decision-
making process when it is needed to demonstrate your performance across
a broader range of teaching roles and activities.

Conversely, underreliance on ratings is a problem that occurs when ratings are ignored. It is not uncommon for administrators to collect ratings
for the appearance of objectivity, but then effectively set them aside, basing
decisions on faculty reputation or students' written comments, particularly
when the reviewers are not comfortable using numbers or doubt the validity of ratings. This is probably more likely to occur when administrators or
committees receive quantitative summaries of ratings items along with students' written comments. Reviewers appear to gravitate toward students'
written comments because they appear richer and more readily interpretable. You may need to explain why the opinions of the majority of the
class as reflected in the ratings should outweigh the articulate but negative
written comments of one or two students. My views on the use of written
comments in personnel decision-making processes can be found in a posi-
tion paper written to advise faculty at my campus:

> Summarizing raw written comments necessarily requires interpretation, para-
> phrasing, and reduction. Different interpreters often understand single writ-

ten comments and patterns of comments differently. Without a strategy for interpreting written comments, subjectivity can easily distort interpretations, especially when the evaluators know the person being evaluated. Evaluators may be unduly influenced by a single highly articulate opinion, positive or negative. The use of multiple readers and systematic content analysis methods can address the reliability problem; however their implementation requires skill and resources [Franklin and Berman, 1997].

If your ratings are strong and will help your case but are being ignored, your ability to decode your ratings for your readers and persuasively connect them to fundamental validity arguments grounded in ratings research may put your ratings back on the table. The challenge is to make the data speak. (See the article "Making Sense of Student Written Comments" in this volume for a discussion of how to analyze written comments.)

Bad Ratings Data. Bad data are data that are potentially misleading or uninformative because the questionnaire used to obtain them was badly constructed, inappropriate to the situation, or administered incorrectly or because the data have been processed, analyzed, or reported incorrectly. If you believe your ratings data are suspect due to such a problem and might result in or contribute to an adverse personnel action, a careful analysis of the problem in your narrative might put reviewers on notice not to overrely on the data. First consider that bad data can come from any or all of these sources: a badly constructed questionnaire, improper administration of the questionnaire, or errors in data processing or analysis.

Questionnaire Construction. Locally constructed questionnaires vary dramatically in quality. Unless the department or institution uses a professionally developed, nationally known rating questionnaire with published validity and reliability data, or perhaps consulted with ratings experts to develop the campus ratings system, do not assume your questionnaire is a good one or that all of the items in it are working as they were intended. Look for a technical report if the questionnaire was institutionally constructed.[1] If reading validation reports of survey instruments is not in your area of expertise, enlist a colleague in a discipline that includes survey research to help you. If your questionnaire has not been assessed for validity and reliability and you are concerned that it has problems that may be causing harm to faculty careers, contact a professional with expertise in ratings for advice. Familiarity with survey methodology alone is not sufficient; familiarity with student ratings as a measure of teaching performance is needed.

Common problems include technical areas such as poorly constructed item stems (questions). An example is the common double-barreled item, which asks two questions at the same time—for example, "Rate the assignments and the exams." Other problems include overly complex or ambiguous stems or poorly scaled response options. Another common problem stems from questions that are irrelevant to good teaching or that students are not well suited to answer. Detecting the latter requires a careful reading of the literature, such as the sources recommended in this article. Do not assume that because you teach, you know what questions should be asked of students.

Questionnaire Administration. Improperly administered ratings questionnaires can result in badly skewed data or even data that have been tampered with. In the case of paper questionnaires, end-of-term ratings should be administered during a class well before exam week begins and by a member of that class while the instructor is out of the room. The instructor should refrain from making prejudicial introductory remarks. Students should be cautioned not to discuss their responses with each other at least until after all forms have been turned in. The forms should be returned by the students unsigned in a sealed envelope to an independent, secure location, and no results should be reported to the instructor until after grades have been filed.

The identity of the student monitor should be recorded. In addition to maintaining student anonymity, students should be informed that their responses are confidential and that the instructor will see only grouped anonymous data. Otherwise, students have a strong incentive to inflate their ratings. If there is a comment section on the form and the whole form goes back to the teacher, students will be concerned that their handwriting may be recognized, and therefore neither their ratings nor their comments are anonymous.

A new technique, administering questionnaires by computer synchronously in a computer lab or asynchronously using Web-based forms, may have a variety of problems related to administration, depending on how it is implemented. Although there is some preliminary evidence that a well-constructed form can successfully be delivered on-line, I believe there are many potential problems, and it is premature to conclude that the paper and computer methods are equivalent. This raises questions for performance appraisal, a process that requires consistency for fairness sake. Moreover, unvalidated Web delivered ratings questionnaires are still that: unvalidated.

Errors in Data Processing or Analysis. No matter how well a questionnaire is constructed or administered, there is one last opportunity for getting bad data: incorrect data or summaries of data resulting from data processing errors, errors of calculation, and programmatic errors causing the wrong information to be printed on reports. The gold standard for checking results is to have the original answer sheets and recalculate questionable results by hand. At a minimum, you should look at your reports with a critical eye. Do not take accuracy for granted. Remember that the computers that produce your report were programmed by humans.

Misinterpretation of Ratings Data. The sources and types of misinterpretation are as varied as there are interpreters. It is beyond the scope of this article to identify more than a few things to watch out for, but in my experience errors fall in three general categories: errors of statistical understanding, unfounded generalizations about the characteristics of ratings, and a general lack of applicable information about effective teaching practices and course design.

Evaluating Your Ratings Data

Making a realistic assessment of the generalizability of your ratings is an essential first step; errors of interpretation typically start with a failure to consider whether the questions were appropriate in the first place or data collected are consistent enough to support any conclusions at all. Take time to study the questionnaire used to collect your ratings, how it was administered, and how the results have been summarized before you begin to draw inferences about your teaching from the data.

The primary concerns are validity (whether the questionnaire measures teaching effectiveness directly or indirectly) and reliability (how faithfully it measures your teaching effectiveness across the many students who responded and the many classes that were rated). Generalizing from the ratings data you have to the larger questions such as how well you teach or how good your course is requires answering questions such as these:

Was the questionnaire well constructed and suitable for use in your course?
How representative of your students' views are these data?
How well do they agree with each other?
Looking across your courses, do you have enough data from enough courses to generalize about your overall teaching effectiveness or your teaching effectiveness within various areas of your teaching load?
Were the data collected and analyzed correctly?

If you suspect any problems in this area, consider addressing them in your narrative if you are concerned that your ratings may have a negative influence on your performance appraisal.

Validity. The validity of the questionnaire is determined by the nature of the questions it asks, as well as how and to whom it is administered. Are the questions singly and as a set capable of measuring what they purport to measure? For example, if a question asks about a characteristic of a teacher, it must have a foundation in research showing a clear connection between that characteristic and teaching effectiveness, and students must be capable of observing that characteristic. If you want to ascertain the potential validity of a ratings questionnaire, the surest way is to consult a source such as Doyle (1983) or an expert on ratings. That said, give or take an item or two, most questionnaires are probably acceptable, assuming that they are not the only source of data.

Reliability. Many of the most egregious errors seem to occur in the willingness of decision makers to rely on data that cannot be assumed to be representative of your average or typical teaching performance. A key concept behind using ratings from one or more courses is that the ratings obtained should be generally representative of your teaching in that particular kind of course. You do not need ratings from every course if you have enough samples of your ratings from which to generalize reliably. What is the likelihood that an item would yield the same results when administered on separate occasions under similar circumstances? How consistent are the results in each class or from class to class? Nearly everyone who has taught long enough has experienced a course that went unusually well and has also been disappointed by a course. Depending on how many courses you have taught and how many courses' worth of ratings are at hand, simply averaging the results may or may not be representative of your results. Every mean score based on an average of many responses to a single question likely is composed of two parts: your hypothetical "true" score and the "error" in measurement.

There are many reasons that "error" can happen:

• The courses or the students within the courses may differ in ways that are likely to be associated with systematic differences in ratings. For example, having an unusually large number of graduate students in an upper-level course one semester could make a difference in the results because graduate students tend to rate faculty higher than do undergraduates, all other things being equal.

• There may not be enough courses to calculate what is typical. This is complicated by the size of the classes. It takes many more instances of small classes to constitute a representative sample than it does for larger classes because as the number of observations (student ratings) increases, the more closely the mean of those ratings will approach a true score. Obviously, the impact of one student's accidentally marking the wrong bubble on the average of all students' ratings is far less in a class of fifty than in a class of five.

• There may not be enough students responding compared to total class enrollment within one or more of the courses, making the results from those courses not representative of all the students in the courses. Generally, the higher the proportion of respondents to students enrolled, the more reliable the results will tend to be, and, at the same time, the smaller the class enrollment, the higher that proportion will need to be to ensure that the sample is reasonably representative. Table 9.1 provides a set of rough guidelines for determining if a reasonably adequate sample has been obtained.

• Averaged results from comparable courses taken over several semesters are likely to be considerably more reliable for comparisons than those from single courses. The number of courses required to construct "average" results increases as the class size decreases. Generally, five or more courses are recommended in most cases, although very small classes certainly need more. For example, courses with as few as five students may need twenty sections for comparison (Centra, 1993).

Table 9.1. Recommended Ratings Response Rates

Class size	Recommended Response[a]
5–20	At least 80 percent; more recommended
20–30	At least 75 percent; more recommended
30–50	At least 66 percent; 75 percent or more recommended
50 or more	At least 60 percent, 75 percent, or more recommended
100 or more	More than 50 percent, 75 percent, or more recommended

[a] Assuming there is no systematic reason that students were absent, the impact of absence on results is larger in smaller classes.

Source: Franklin and Theall (1991).

Reliability is a complex subject, and unless you are comfortable with the vocabulary and methods of this kind of analysis, I recommend focusing on two aspects of your data:

- How good the sample of your work is based on the proportion of students responding to the questionnaire in each class and the proportion of your classes (overall teaching load) in which ratings were collected
- The consistency with which your students responded in each class and from class to class

Comparing Scores Among Classes or Across Faculty. One of the most problematic areas in the use of ratings is comparison of raw mean scores among faculty or against some other kind of implicit or explicit normative standard. Comparisons are often made explicitly (for example, 3.4 versus 3.5) or implicitly based on the reviewer's personal opinions about where to draw the boundaries (for example, 3.0 is bad, and 3.5 is okay). The difficulty with either approach is that the problem of error in ratings and its effects on ratings means is ignored. Your challenge in the narrative is to put the issue of precision back on the table.

Remember that ratings usually include some error from mismarks, misreads, or less-than-optimum sampling; they are not precise. One of the most common errors of ratings interpretation is the use of raw mean scores as precise indicators of teaching effectiveness. Your task in a narrative is to remind the raters of the level of precision (or imprecision) of those means to discourage erroneous conclusions about what the means indicate. This can be done by showing the margin of error of each item and the confidence interval within which the true score probably lies. Following is a simplified method for calculating the margin of error and the confidence interval (Doyle, 1983):

1. You will need an item's mean, standard deviation (SD), and the number of students responding to that item (n). These numbers should be

supplied by the survey administrators. As an example, for Item 2, the mean is 4.4, SD is 0.52, and n is 10.

2. Divide the SD by the square root of n. This is the standard error of the mean (how much the mean is likely to vary)—for example, 0.52/3.62 [the square root of 10] = .16 (rounded to two decimal places).

3. Multiply the standard error of the mean obtained in Step 2 by 1.96 (a statistically based constant) to get the actual amount the mean might vary: .16 × 1.96 = .31.

4. To get the 95 percent confidence interval, subtract the amount calculated in Step 3 from the mean to get the lowest probable limit of your true score. Then add the amount calculated in Step 3 to the mean to get the highest probable limit of your true score. This range from the lowest probable limit to the highest probable limit is the 95 percent confidence interval. Your true score on that item will fall within this interval with a 95 percent probability—for example, lowest level = 4.4 − .31 = 4.09; highest level = 4.4 + .31 = 4.71. The true score lies somewhere between 4.09 and 4.71.

This means that if the confidence interval spans a really large range of scores, the precision of that item is suspect; your true score could be anywhere in that interval. If the confidence interval is a narrow range of scores, the item is a better measure from a precision standpoint.

If the thought of calculating these values sends shivers down your spine, find an agreeable colleague or graduate student knowledgeable about statistics to help you compute and understand them before you write your narrative. But do understand them!

Comparing Your Results to Those of Others. Even if you know where your own score most likely falls, it is not safe to conclude that two apparently different means (for example, your own and that of the overall department) are necessarily statistically different. The apparent difference may be the result of chance or systematic error. However, having established the precision of your own results, you can then compare them with any norm or benchmark for ratings. If you have the standard deviation and number of courses for the overall department mean, you can compute the 95 percent confidence interval of that mean as well. Using the procedure just outlined, but with the mean and standard deviation for the overall department group instead of the your mean and standard deviation and substituting the number of courses in the overall department group for the number of student responses you used before, compute a confidence interval for the overall department mean on the same item. This allows you to compare your data with the overall department mean.

One useful approach is to make a table (Table 9.2) showing your results compared with the department results and even indicate each time that your results are significantly higher than, at the same level as, or significantly lower than the department mean for the same item. In this example, your narrative might say, "During the period from spring 1998 through spring

Table 9.2. Summarizing Means and Confidence Intervals

The comparison group is all upper-division undergraduate courses in English with fewer than 20 students enrolled (1995–1998): 148 sections with 3,077 student responses

Course	Term	Enrolled versus Responded	My Overall Effectiveness Rating (Item 2)		Comparison Group (overall department) Effectiveness Ratings (item 2)		Contrast: My Mean versus the Comparison Mean at 95 Percent Probability
			Mean	95 Percent Confidence Interval	Mean	95 Percent Confidence Interval	
ENG 483-002	SP-96	7/7	4.86	4.51–5.00	4.11	4.01–4.21	Significantly higher
ENG 452-001	FA-96	12/10	4.80	4.50–5.00			Significantly higher
ENG 452-001	SP-97	10/8	4.63	4.19–5.00			Marginally higher
ENG-452-002	SP-97	8/7	4.29	3.26–5.00			Not significantly different
ENG-497B-597	FA-97						(No ratings available)
ENG-483-002	SP-98	11/11	4.91	4.71–5.00			Significantly higher

2000, I taught six upper-division courses, for which student ratings were collected in five of six sections. (The student monitor lost the package in the sixth section; see the note from the student.) My ratings of instructional effectiveness were higher than the department average for similar courses based on size and level four out of five times." The important point for this narrative is that you have a statistically sound basis for concluding that your ratings are truly higher, or not different from, or truly lower than whatever standard for comparison is being used.

Mitigating Circumstances and What Makes a Difference. Whatever the comparison approach your evaluators may take, in order to make valid, useful comparisons among items, instructors, or sections, any comparisons should also take into account the following dictum: the more similar the classes or sections being compared (in terms of, say, content, level of the students, class size, or prerequisite versus elective), the more valid the comparison is. However, in practice, another area of serious concern should be whether the ratings users know what characteristics of teachers, students, and courses have actually been shown to be correlated with ratings. (Good sources for this kind of information include Doyle, 1983; Feldman, 1978; Braskamp and Ory, 1994; Centra, 1993.)

Here are some things that research suggests may influence ratings, along with some suggestions about them:

• Years of teaching experience. This factor has a predictable (and intuitively logical) influence on ratings that should be taken into consideration when comparing scores. The poorest ratings are usually obtained by instructors with less than one year of experience. Teachers with between three and twelve years of experience tend to receive the best ratings, and those with one to two years or more than twelve years receive relatively intermediate ratings. If you are in the early stages of your career, this may be a useful fact to point out.

• Class size. Students tend to rank instructors who are teaching small classes (fewer than twenty students) most highly, followed by those with around twenty to forty students. The lowest ratings seem to occur in large classes with forty to sixty or so students, but ratings are slightly higher again for extremely large classes, especially those larger than one hundred students. (I suspect that students abandon expectations for personal contact when classes are very large, but still hold faculty to them in large classes where personal contact may be possible but difficult.) If your institution uses norms or comparison data that do not control for class size, use your narrative to point out this problem if your ratings are lower than the comparison ratings.

• Electives. Students tend to give slightly higher ratings to their majors or electives than to courses taken to fulfill a requirement. If your teaching load is on the required side and your results are consistently compared with results from predominantly elective courses, you should point out the need for a better match for comparison purposes.

• Discipline. Courses in the humanities tend to be rated more highly than those in the physical sciences and engineering, with social and behavioral sciences falling in between. Courses with a concern for practice are rated higher than courses with a strong theoretical orientation. A variety of other disciplinary differences have also been observed. Most sources agree that ratings should not be compared across disciplines. If comparisons are necessary, it is preferable to compare the standings of faculty within their own disciplinary comparison groups. Of all the factors that could work to the advantage or disadvantage of faculty, this is one of the most important. If your ratings are compared to a schoolwide mean or to comparison groups that include courses outside your discipline in the broadest sense, be prepared to challenge this in your narrative.

• Innovation. New or revised courses frequently get lower-than-expected ratings the first time out. This may be very important if you have been active in developing or revising a course for which you do not have abundant ratings. New courses make take time to work the bugs out, and consequently you may have lower ratings than usual. In your narrative, point out that the course is new; then take a positive tack and describe how the ratings are helping you fine-tune or revise the course.

Some factors rarely influence ratings:

• Schedule. Time of day and scheduling factors within a semester appear to have little or no influence on ratings. However, there may be systematic differences in who attends classes at particular times, which may have some impact on ratings. One important exception is that summer session courses frequently receive higher ratings than comparable fall or spring counterparts, so avoid comparing summer data with main academic year data.

• Student ability. Academic ability of students as measured by grade point average has shown little relationship to the ratings they give; students who do poorly are just as appreciative of good teaching as students who do well, and students who do well are just as critical of poor teaching as are less able students and perhaps a little more so (Theall and Franklin, 1990). Do not fall victim to the self-serving canard that your good students gave you the highest ratings. Unless your data have been cross-tabulated and show that this was the case in your·class, it is only speculation. Moreover, from another point of view, how well you teach the students who need you the most is also a measure of your teaching skill.

The following factors have a more complex (and often ambiguous) relationship to ratings include:

• Workload and difficulty. Workload and course difficulty deserve special consideration. I have heard too many faculty and administrators dismiss the low ratings of a colleague because he or she also had a reputation for being tough on students or, conversely, that a highly rated teacher's ratings must have been due to a lack of substance or challenge in the course. Although getting high ratings for a challenging course is commendable and should be pointed out in your narrative, in the absence of high ratings, perceived difficulty could actually result from poor teaching and a heavy workload. Although "academic rigor" is a common excuse for low ratings, it is not by itself a sign of good teaching. Only a careful look by qualified peers at a course's content, assignments, exams, and grading policy can determine if the level of challenge was instructionally appropriate.

• Grades and ratings. There is a moderate positive correlation between ratings and expected course grades, although this alone does not demonstrate that ratings are biased by grades. There is a logical relationship between student satisfaction at anticipating higher grades and the ratings they give. Good teachers have successful students who rate their teachers highly. This does not mean than an individual instructor will attempt to "buy" better ratings by reducing the work or challenge needed to earn a grade. Many faculty are concerned about the possibility that the rise in the use of ratings has caused widespread grade inflation. This may or may not be true. If it has, it is because faculty gave higher grades, not because students gave higher ratings. Giving students unearned good grades and reducing the effort needed to earn grades have been demonstrated to have virtually no payoff for raising ratings in the long run, provided ratings are anonymous. Also, having a clear and fair grading policy is one aspect of good teaching. Being a tough grader does not by itself signify good teaching. This concern is outside the purview of ratings as a measure of teaching performance and is better served by attention from curriculum and instruction committees by regular review of grade distributions.

When writing a narrative, it is useful to know which factors have been shown to have some relationship to ratings and which have not. It is also useful to know that the significant associations between such variables and ratings when they do occur are mostly weak ones and usually would not make a noticeable difference in your ratings. One of the most natural things to do when reading evaluations of one's own performance, especially when they are less than stellar, is to challenge the results by looking for reasons that the evaluations were wrong or biased by factors not under our control. It is in this area that misconceptions and mythology about ratings abound.

Pulling It All Together: Ratings and the Scholarship of Teaching

Understanding the basics about ratings is very helpful in interpreting them. That may seem too obvious to say, but I have learned not to take this for granted. When misused, they may actually short-circuit useful discourse, so it is alarming to see how many faculty and administrators lacking critical skills and information about ratings use them routinely to evaluate teaching performance. Whatever the cause, ratings are not doing as good a job as they should in informing decisions that affect the careers of faculty. Nor are faculty using them as productively as they might in informing their own teaching practices. The causes for poor practice are complex and many, but the remedy offered by faculty educating themselves about good practices for using ratings data works on many levels.

When data from well-constructed ratings questionnaires become just one valued source of information among many in faculty evaluation and personnel decision-making processes, they can fuel active inquiry, reflection, and practice for faculty, and they will cease to do the harm that has discredited them so often among faculty. An article such as this can point you in the right direction, but a deeper reading can also serve you well, depending on how much you have at stake when ratings are used in evaluating your performance as a teacher. At minimum, it can help you seek out and identify sources of expert advice if it is needed. In the long run, the reflection required to construct a narrative analysis of your ratings offers an opportunity to engage in what we so often espouse for our students: active learning, that is, learning about teaching.

Note

1. A good example of such a report and an exemplary ratings system can be seen on the Web site of the Office of Educational Assessment at the University of Washington: www.washington.edu/oea/ias1.htm.

References

Arreola, R. A. *Developing a Comprehensive Faculty Evaluation System.* Bolton, Mass.: Anker, 2000.
Braskamp, L. A., and Ory, J. C. *Assessing Faculty Work.* San Francisco: Jossey-Bass, 1994.
Centra, J. A. *Reflective Faculty Evaluation.* San Francisco: Jossey-Bass, 1993.
Doyle, K. O. *Evaluating Teaching.* San Francisco: New Lexington Press, 1983.
Feldman, K. A. "Course Characteristics and College Students' Ratings of Their Teachers and Courses: What We Know and What We Don't." *Research in Higher Education,* 1978, *9,* 199–242.
Franklin, J., and Berman, E. "Using Student Written Comments in Summative Evaluation." In *University of Arizona Administrators' Guide to Using TCE Results.* Tucson: University of Arizona, Office of Instructional Assessment and Evaluation, 1997.
Franklin, J., and Theall, M. "Rating the Readers: Knowledge, Attitudes, and Practices of Users of Student Ratings of Instruction." Paper presented at the Seventy-Fourth Annual Meeting of the American Educational Research Association, San Francisco, Apr. 1989.
Lewis, K. G., and Lunde, J. P. *Face to Face: A Sourcebook of Individual Consultation Techniques for Faculty/Instructional Developers.* Stillwater, Okla.: New Forums Press, 2001.
Seldin, P. *The Teaching Portfolio.* Bolton, Mass.: Anker, 1984.
Theall, M., and Franklin, J. (eds.), "Student Ratings of Instruction: Issues for Improving Practice." New Directions for Teaching and Learning, no. 43. San Francisco: Jossey-Bass, 1990.

Theall, M., and Franklin, J. "If I Had a Hammer: Some Thoughts on Appropriately Using Technology to Facilitate Evaluation." In P. Cranton and C. Knapper (eds.), *Fresh Approaches to Teaching Evaluation*. New Directions for Teaching and Learning, no. 87. San Francisco: Jossey-Bass, in press.

JENNIFER FRANKLIN is director of the Center for Teaching and Learning at California State University, Dominguez Hills.

INDEX

Abrami, P. C., 6, 7, 9
Active learning techniques, 40
Aleamoni, L. M., 4
Angelo, T., 38, 45, 46, 47, 49, 50, 56, 78
Anonymity, 7, 18, 90
Argulewiz, E., 7
Assessment questions: direct versus self-report, 77–78; learning objectives and, 79–80, 82–83; open- versus closed-ended, 78–79; as opportunity for student reflection, 81–82; writing guidelines for, 79–83

Bandura, A., 20
Basow, S. A., 6
Batista, E. E., 6
Bausell, C. R., 4
Bausell, R. B., 4
Bennett, S. K., 6
Berman, E., 89
Bernard, M. E., 6
Bias studies, 9
Billson, J. M., 74, 75
Blackburn, R. T., 9
Bloom, B. S., 80
Bowers, N., 45
Brandenburg, D. C., 6, 9
Brashamp, L. A., 8, 9, 12, 18, 96

Cappe, L., 18
Cashin, W. E., 5, 8, 63
Caulley, D. N., 9
Centra, J. A., 5, 6, 7, 8, 9, 12, 92, 96
Check, J., 6
Chiu, S., 5
Clark, M. J., 9
Class size, as influence on student ratings, 5, 96
Classroom assessment techniques (CATs), 38–39, 45
Classroom Reaction Survey, 34, 39
Cohen, P. A., 9, 29
Comprehensive Faculty Evaluation System, 87
Confidentiality, 90
Conway, C. G., 9
Cook, J. A., 6
Cooper, T., 6
Corbin, J., 73

Costin, F., 4, 9
Course difficulty, as influence on student ratings, 98
Course level, as influence on student ratings, 4–5
Creech, F. R., 6
Critical reflection, induced by assessment questions, 81–82
Cross, K. P., 38
Cross, P., 45, 46, 47, 49, 50, 56, 78

d'Apollonia, S., 9
Dickens, W. J., 7
Dienst, E. R., 29
Dimensionality studies, 9–10
Discipline, as influence on student ratings, 5, 97
Doyle, K. G., Jr., 6, 8
Doyle, K. O., 96

Elective courses, as influence on student ratings, 4, 5, 96–97
Elsworth, G., 6
Erdle, ?, 4
Evaluation process: active learning techniques in, 40; classroom assessment techniques (CATs) in, 38–39, 45; in classroom survey, 34–38; desirable characteristics of, 33–35; midsemester, 38–44; one-minute papers in, 38; and responses to students, 39–42

Faculty evaluation plan, evaluation of, 86–88. See also Student feedback; Student ratings
Faculty productivity, as influence on student ratings, 6
Feldman, K. A., 4, 5, 6, 7, 8, 9, 29, 96
Ferber, M. A., 6
Focus group(s), 63–75; consensus and, 67; contradictory feedback and, 64; questioning technique in, 64–66; strengths and weaknesses of, 73–75; summaries of, teacher's reactions to, 68–72; summarizing and checking process in, 66–72; transcript analysis, 72–73
Franklin, J., 5, 8, 31, 85, 86, 89, 92, 93, 97
Fuhrman, B. S., 33

SINGLE ISSUE SALE

For a limited time save 10% on single issues! Save an additional 10% when you purchase three or more single issues. Each issue is normally $27^{00}.

Please see the next page for a complete listing of available back issues.

Mail or fax this completed form to: Jossey-Bass, A Wiley Company
989 Market Street • Fifth Floor • San Francisco CA 94103-1741

CALL OR FAX

Phone **888-378-2537** or **415-433-1740** *or Fax* **800-605-2665** or **415-433-4611** (*attn customer service*)
    BE SURE TO USE PROMOTION CODE **ND2** TO GUARANTEE YOUR DISCOUNT!
Please send me the following issues at $24^{30} each.

(Important: please include series initials and issue number, such as TL86)

1. TL _____

_____

$ _____Total for single issues ($24^{30} each)

_____Less 10% if ordering 3 or more issues

_____Shipping charges: Up to $30, add $5^{50} • $30^{01} –$50, add $6^{50}
$50^{01} –$75, add $7^{50} • $75^{01} –$100, add $9^{00} • $100^{01} –$150, add $10^{00}
Over $150, call for shipping charge.

$ _____Total (Add appropriate sales tax for your state. Canadian residents add GST)

❑ Payment enclosed (U.S. check or money order only)

❑ VISA, MC, AmEx Discover Card # _____ Exp. date _____

Signature _____

Day phone _____

❑ Bill me (U.S. institutional orders only. Purchase order required)
Purchase order # _____
     Federal Tax ID. 135593032   GST 89102 8052

Name _____

Address _____

_____

Phone _____ E-mail _____
For more information about Jossey-Bass, visit our website at: www.josseybass.com

OFFER EXPIRES FEBRUARY 28, 2002.   **PRIORITY CODE = ND2**

Save Now on the Best of ABOUT CAMPUS Series Sets
Enriching the Student Learning Experience

Dedicated to the idea that student learning is the responsibility of all educators on campus, **About Campus** illuminates critical issues faced by both student affairs and academic affairs staff as they work on the shared goal that brought them to the same campus in the first place: to help students learn.

With each issue, **About Campus** combines the imagination and creativity found in the best magazines and the authority and thoughtfulness found in the best professional journals. Now we've taken the four most popular issues from three volume years and we've made them available as a set— at a tremendous savings over our $20.00 single issue price.

Best of About Campus – Volume 3

Facts and Myths About Assessment in Student Affairs – Why Learning Communities? Why Now? – The Stressed Student: How Can We Help? – Being All That We Can Be
ISBN 0–7879–6128–0 $12.00

Best of About Campus – Volume 4

Increasing Expectations for Student Effort – The Matthew Shepard Tragedy: Crisis and Beyond – Civic and Moral Learning – Faculty-Student Affairs Collaboration on Assessment.
ISBN 0–7879–6129–9 $12.00

Best of About Campus – Volume 5

The Diversity Within – What Can We Do About Student Cheating – Bonfire: Tragedy and Tradition – Hogwarts: The Learning Community.
ISBN 0–7879–6130–2 $12.00

To order by phone: call 1–800–956–7739 or 415–433–1740

Visit our website at www.josseybass.com

Use promotion code **ND2** to guarantee your savings.
Shipping and applicable taxes will be added.

ABOUT CAMPUS

Sponsored by the *American College Personnel Association*
Published by Jossey-Bass, A Wiley Company

Patricia M. King, Executive Editor
Jon C. Dalton, Senior Editor

Published bimonthly. Individual subscriptions $53.00. Institutional subscriptions $95.00.

Jossey-Bass, A Wiley Company • 989 Market St., Fifth Floor • San Francisco, CA 94103–1741

learners. Explains how to use each assessment measure presented, including developing criteria, integrating peer and self-assessment, and assigning grades.

TL73   **Academic Service Learning: A Pedagogy of Action and Reflection**
Robert A. Rhoads, Jeffrey P.F. Howard
Presents an academic conception of service learning, described as "a pedagogical model that intentionally integrates academic learning and relevant community service." Describes successful programs, and discusses issues that faculty and administrators must consider as they incorporate service into courses and curricula.

TL72   **Universal Challenges in Faculty Work: Fresh Perspectives from Around the World**
Patricia Cranton
Educators from around the world describe issues they face in their teaching practice. National differences are put into the context of universal themes including responding to demands for social development and reacting to influences by government policies and financial constraints.

TL71   **Teaching and Learning at a Distance: What It Takes to Effectively Design, Deliver, and Evaluate Programs**
Thomas E. Cyrs
Offers insights from experienced practitioners into what is needed to make teaching and learning at a distance successful for everyone involved.

TL70   **Approaches to Teaching Non-Native English Speakers Across the Curriculum**
David L. Sigsbee, Bruce W. Speck, Bruce Maylath
Provides strategies that help students who are non-native users of English improve their writing and speaking skills in content-area courses. Considers the points of view of the students themselves and discusses their differing levels of intent about becoming proficient in English writing and speaking.

TL69   **Writing to Learn: Strategies for Assigning and Responding to Writing Across the Disciplines**
Mary Deane Sorcinelli, Peter Elbow
Presents strategies and philosophies about the way writing is learned, both in the context of a discipline and as an independent skill. Focusing primarily on the best ways to give feedback about written work, the authors describe a host of alternatives that have a solid foundation in research.

TL68   **Bringing Problem-Based Learning to Higher Education: Theory and Practice**
LuAnn Wilkerson, Wim H. Gijselaers
Describes the basics of problem-based learning, along with the variables that affect its success. Provides examples of its application in a wide range of disciplines, including medicine, business, education, engineering, mathematics, and the sciences.

TL67   **Using Active Learning in College Classes: A Range of Options for Faculty**
Tracey E. Sutherland, Charles C. Bonwell
Examines the use of active learning in higher education and describes the concept of the active learning continuum, tying various practical examples of active learning to that concept.